The Communion of Saints

a

The
Communion of Saints

BY THE
REV. WYLLYS REDE, D.D.
RECTOR OF EMMANUEL CHURCH, ROCHFORD

WITH AN INTRODUCTION BY
LORD HALIFAX

"Angels and living Saints and dead
But one communion make."
"Knit together in one communion and fellowship in the mystical Body of
Christ."

SECOND EDITION

LONGMANS, GREEN, & CO.
LONDON, NEW YORK, AND BOMBAY
1896
All rights reserved

TO

MY PARENTS

WHOM

TAKEN FROM ME IN MY INFANCY

I HAVE KNOWN

ONLY IN

THE COMMUNION OF SAINTS.

INTRODUCTION

BY THE

RIGHT HON. VISCOUNT HALIFAX

FAITH which does not express itself in act soon ceases to exist. Belief which does not result in practice ceases soon to be any belief at all. It is for this reason, among others, that the practice of the Church has such an important bearing on doctrine. The practice of the Church enshrines, preserves, and perpetuates her doctrine, and to suppose that the one can be divorced from the other, that the faith can be maintained without the practice which gives it expression, is to contradict the general experience of mankind at large.

An illustration of this may be found in the doctrine of the Communion of Saints, which is the subject of the following pages.

The Communion of Saints is an article of the Creed; as such it is recited day by day, often several times in the day, by most members of the Anglican Communion; and yet will any one deny, article of the Creed though it be, that to a vast number of the members of the English Church and of Churches in visible communion with her, it is anything else but the merest dead letter?

It was not always so. There may have been in times past exaggeration; there may even have been superstition;

beliefs and practices may have been taught and insisted upon as certainly true and resting upon the same foundation as the Creeds themselves, which, whether true or not, could not rightly claim more than the authority of private opinions; but the fact remains that as long as the Church of England gave a fuller and more explicit expression to her belief in the Communion of Saints, in her public worship and by the devotions she inculcated upon her children, so long that belief maintained itself. Since she has only done so implicitly, and has to so great an extent withdrawn the more definite expression of the doctrine from the public worship and practice of her children, it has withered away, and been well nigh ready to perish altogether.

No doubt it would be unfair to assert
that the reserve and silence exhibited
by the public services of the Church of
England, and what has been the general
attitude of her members on the subject,
are alone responsible for the neglect into
which the doctrine of the Communion of
Saints has fallen among those who belong
to the Anglican body.   Something—a
great deal, perhaps—is due to defective
views of the Incarnation itself, the result
of ignorance of the Church's teaching.
Those who ignore that what constitutes
Christ's claim to act on our behalf, and
invests Him as our Representative, with
the right and power to make atonement
for sin and to reconcile mankind to God,
is His real participation in the nature
of those for whom He acts, are not likely

to realize the links which bind the
members of Christ's Body to their Head
and to one another. But making every
allowance for the consequences of such
defective teaching, can we deny that the
doctrine of the Communion of Saints is to
too many at the present day a doctrine
of which they have no intelligent con-
ception, with which they have no practical concern ; and that the fact is largely
due to the changes made in the public
services of the Church in the sixteenth
century, and the consequent decline of
practice and observance by which that
doctrine had expressed itself in act ?
What is the attitude of large numbers
of persons in regard to the departed ?
Is it not one of silence or unreality ?—
of unreality and worse than unreality

when the departed are spoken of with
an assurance which nothing in their
past lives can warrant; of silence when
death, as is too often the case, is felt to
be a wall of separation, precluding all
fellowship and communion with those
who have entered within the veil? To
such persons death seems the end of all
things. They believe in, and vaguely
hope for, heaven; they also believe in,
and vaguely dread, the possibility of hell.
They hope, less vaguely, perhaps, for a
meeting hereafter with those they have
loved and lost, for here the instinctive
teaching of the human heart is too
strong for defective theology; but to
all intents and purposes their dead are
dead indeed. They are buried out
of sight, the link that bound them to

the living is snapped; they who remain can do no more for those who are gone, and the best thing that is left is to put away, in the tumult and distractions of life, all thought of those the remembrance of whom brings with it nothing but a fruitless yearning or an aching pain.

This little book is an attempt to contribute something towards a happier and more primitive belief and practice amongst members of the Anglican Communion. It is an attempt to show that in the Body of Christ death snaps no links that bind souls together, but rather draws them closer than before.

It insists, in accordance with the teaching of the Universal Church, that, whether living in the flesh on this visible earth, or as disembodied spirits waiting for the restitution of all things, as members of the one Body, what touches one touches all; that between earth and heaven there is a constant and unbroken communion, a constant interchange of good offices and good works.

The ladder seen by the patriarch in vision has not been withdrawn between heaven and earth, and the angels of God ascend and descend in very deed and truth upon the members of the Body of the Son of Man, the children of the Second Adam, the members of the redeemed and ransomed race. Hemmed in by the body of this flesh, limited by time and hampered by space, the Faithful who are still on earth may be in various degrees unconscious of their

fellowship with those within the veil;
but the fellowship exists, and supplies a
motive for present action and abiding
work.

Translated for no merit of our own,
but by God's free grace, into the kingdom of His dear Son, as members of the
family of God, what love prompts one
to do or to suffer, has an availing power
with God for all.

That soul we loved as ourselves, every
thought connected with whom is full
of joy and peace; or that other who it
may be seemed to the very last to
neglect the call of Christ, how can it be
that we should forget them in our thanks-
givings and our prayers, or that the
intercessions and offerings we make on
their behalf should not have power

to prevail with God, our Father and theirs ?

It is not our worthiness, but our love, which pleads for all souls with their Maker and ours. Love, even in this lower world, and as between man and man, has power to undo the past. Has it less power between man and God ? "See," we cry to God, "these prayers, these alms, these acts of self-denial. It is not so much we who offer them, but we in the place of, and as the mouthpiece of, these Thy servants—our brother, sister, parent, child. In the place of this friend we have loved as our own selves, of this other we have injured, and for whom we would now make the only reparation in our power. Nay, it is they themselves who still plead and

offer through us, by whose mouth they
still cry, 'Despise not Thou, O Lord,
the work of Thine own hands!'"

What is the Office for the Dead; what
is every Eucharist offered on behalf of
the departed, but the dead in Christ,
in the persons of and through the lips
and hands of the living, still pouring out
their own supplications and prayers, and
making their own intercessions and
offerings before the Majesty on high?

And so, too, the blessed Saints, who
reign with Christ, and who follow the
Lamb whithersoever He goeth, they also
are touched by the necessities of the
Body to which they belong. They, too,
are not indifferent to our sorrows and
our perplexities. Those who stand in
the light of God's love, are they less

b

sensible of our needs than we of theirs?
Do they ever cease from their good
offices on our behalf? Shall we on
earth remember them, and they in
heaven forget us? Nay, what we do
for them they do also for us, only how
far more effectually!—there within the
veil, and in the immediate presence of
Him who only waits to be asked, even
by sinners like ourselves, to give more
than we can either hope or think.

But some one will say, "Can the
blessed dead and the saints who rest
in the Paradise of God, can they see
and know, and not be troubled by, the
sights and sins, the sorrows and pangs,
of this lower world? Can Christ have
entered into His glory and His abiding
joy, and yet be touched again by our

infirmities and crucified again by our sins ? " The one question answers the other. It is not a difficulty which need disturb us. Our day, the day of this present life, is a day which is neither dark nor light; but at eventide, at its close, there shall be light. In the dawning of the eternal morning, in that day which shall have no end, all will be made clear, and we shall understand how the rest of Paradise has been undisturbed by the troubles and sins of earth, and yet how the blessed dead, like Moses and Elias on the mount, have had their part and share in all the sufferings, yea, in all the agony and in all the sorrow even unto death, which has in this lower world weighed down the sons of men.

Who, indeed, is there who has not felt
that those we call dead are nearer to us
than the living ? The living are with
us now and again, we are divided from
them by time and space ; but the dead
are with us always, we approach them
when we will, for the dwelling-place
and movements of our spirits depend
not on change of place : where our
hearts are, there are we ourselves.
Much more are the blessed dead un-
fettered by the limitations which hedge
us in who are still in the body. In
that blessed Communion which unites
all members of the Body of Christ to
one another, we have access to them
when we will, we speak to them and
entreat their prayers, we listen to their
holy inspirations, we are conscious of

their guidance and protection, and in the sense of the fellowship begotten of such intercourse we come to know that the Communion of Saints is a fact, not merely to be asserted when we recite the Creed, but a very present help in trouble, and a blessed and most glorious reality which touches this lower world with a radiance which is not its own.

Let us, then, try to think more of the dead in Christ. To think of them purifies our affections, and accustoms us to dwell upon the things that are not seen, rather than those of this visible world, which is so soon, as far as we ourselves are concerned, to pass away. To live in the world unseen is to extend our view beyond the grave into that state where souls live. It is to enter into the gates of the heavenly Jerusalem, to dwell with an innumerable company of angels, and the spirits of just men made perfect. Who can feel alone in the company of the saints ? Who need feel helpless if they are on his side ? Who can tell what their intercession may obtain for us ? Who can estimate how much we may lose if we limit ourselves to the society of the dwellers upon earth, and refuse to hold any intercourse with the inhabitants of heaven ? Above all, let us remember the dead in Christ in our prayers and at the Altar. Let us offer the Holy Sacrifice on their behalf. The Sacrifice of the Altar is one with the abiding offering which our Lord as our great High Priest makes for us in heaven. That heavenly intercession is nothing else than the perpetual offering of the Eternal Victim, who, by His death upon the Cross, made a full, perfect, and sufficient Sacrifice for the sins of the whole world.

Offering Him who has made a satisfaction for all, we offer for all living and departed who have been or ever shall be born into the world; and in the Communion which follows upon the Sacrifice we are brought into fellowship with Him, and with all the members of His Body. It is in this Communion which knits all the members of the Body into one that the doctrine of the Communion of Saints has its root. The members of that Body are partakers of that Spirit who goeth and cometh whithersoever He wills. In the Spirit they live unto God,

and in that life which He imparts they
are free from the trammels of space and
time, and are brought into the company
of the blessed, and to that assembly of
the saints in light, of which the full
glory shall be seen when God shall
finally be revealed, and shall stand once
more upon this earth, and bring all His
saints with Him.

It is by the practice which belief in
such Communion involves, and which
necessarily flows from it, that a living,
operative belief in the article of the
Creed which is the subject of the
present volume, is preserved and se-
cured. May it please Almighty God to
bless the endeavour made by its author
to impart a fuller and deeper knowledge
of that Faith which is our support in

death, and our abiding and never-failing consolation amid all the sorrows and bereavements, the chances and changes, of this mortal life!

HALIFAX.

Hickleton, Doncaster,
October, 1893.

AUTHOR'S PREFACE

THE genesis of this book lies far back in the "long, long thoughts" of boyish years, when its writer was forced (before his time) to face great mysteries and to realize relationships which others do not begin to grasp until later on in life. The convictions which it embodies have had a gradual growth and have been laboriously matured. They first took definite shape in a course of lectures given in St. Mark's Church, Evanston, Illinois, upon the Sunday nights of Lent, 1892, which were received with so many signs of interest that, acting upon the judgment of trusted advisers, the writer determined to put them into print. It has seemed best to hold quite closely to the didactic form which they naturally took at first. It would have been easy to recast them into a more bookish shape, but it was urged that in the process some of their directness of style and cumulativeness of argument would be lost. Of course, this book is not intended as a contribution to the controversial literature of eschatology. It is designed simply to answer as frankly and clearly as may be the questionings of many hearts, to tell busy people in the language of common life what they may consistently hold to be the truth about their relationships in the Church of Christ. Relationships are the strongest things in the universe. Thin and impalpable though they seem, they bind us all like bands of steel. The idea of *relationship* seems to the writer to be the key to the understanding of the life of the unseen world, and his apology for putting these pages into print must be that (so far as he is aware) no one else has made use of it to any considerable extent. If anything should be found

herein contrary to the teaching of the historic
Church of Christ throughout the world, may
God neutralize its powers for harm and make
it of none effect. The writer desires to acknowledge his indebtedness to the Rev.
Professor Gold, of the Western Theological
Seminary at Chicago, for having gone over
the manuscript and given valuable advice.
He sends forth this little book with the hope
that it may help some to realize and appro-
priate the blessings which flow from a devout
belief in the catholic doctrine of the Communion of Saints.

W. R.

Oxford,
    Whitsuntide, 1893.

CONTENTS

CHAPTER I.

WHAT IS THE COMMUNION OF SAINTS?

"A LOST link in the chain of the Church's Creed"—such are the words applied by one of the most gifted writers of modern times to a part of the fifth article of the Apostles' Creed. They would describe with at least equal truth another part of that creed in which we profess our belief in the Communion of Saints. Of that too we might say with him, "We repeat the words, but they do not move us. Our thoughts about them are indistinct and dim. They bring no strength or comfort to us."[1] The doctrine of the Communion of Saints has been neglected altogether too much. We have been too long ignorant of the great depth and fulness of meaning which it holds. We have lost the

[1] Dean Plumptre, *The Spirits in Prison.*

B

help and comfort which a full knowledge of
our relationship to God's saints would most
surely bring to us. A great preacher of the
American Church has been quite warranted
in describing this as "a lost faith, buried
deep by ancient prejudice, ignorance, and
long disuse. The words express many relations, many mysteries ; they stand for a
great network of complicated, involved, con-
fusing, but most precious and blessed truths.
Of these our minds and hearts ought to be
full ; yet we do not comprehend them, we
seldom think of them ; through the unbelief
and impiety of this age, many of them are
as empty words without reality. And yet
they bring the visible and invisible worlds
close together, nay, they make them overlap
each other's boundaries, and extend as it
were into each other." [1] Let us, then, attempt
to exhume this doctrine from the *débris* under
which it was buried by the volcanic activities
of Reformation times, and restore it to its
rightful place in our Christian faith and life.

[1] Dr. Dix, *Sermon on the Communion of Saints.*

The dominant theme in the Christian thought of the fourth century was the Divinity of our Lord ; in the sixteenth it was the redemption of mankind through Christ ; in the nineteenth it is the life beyond the grave. Our age enters with an earnestness and intensity, such as no previous one has felt, into the great questions which concern the future life. Most of these questions find their answer, so far as one is to be found, in the doctrine of the Communion of Saints. It is a doctrine infinitely practical, and able to set at rest inquiries which thrust themselves into the foreground of all human thought, and confront every soul. We shall therefore do well to study it and embody it in our lives. I believe that thus we shall satisfy the cravings—unknown and unexpressed, perhaps, but none the less genuine and strong—of every soul within reach of my words. As we go on we shall encounter problems, some of them deep and hard, before which unassisted human thought staggers and sometimes falls. But we shall view them in the light of God's truth. We

shall have as our Guide and Teacher the
Church of Christ. We shall bring the best
wisdom of the ages to bear upon them. And
so I think we need not fear. I am confident
that an intelligent and reverent study of this
fundamental Christian truth will enlarge and
enrich the grounds of our belief and be most
helpful in the duties of our daily life.

First we shall need to define our terms.
What is the exact meaning of the expression,
"Communion of Saints"?

The word "communion" is not difficult to
define. It means a common share or fellowship. When used in a religious sense, it
means a mystical partnership in some supernatural grace or life. When we speak of the
Holy Communion of the Body and Blood of
Christ, we mean the mystical union with the
divine life of our Lord which is vouchsafed
to us in His blessed sacrament. By the
communion of saints we mean the spiritual
relationship which knits together all God's
saints in the mystical Body of Christ.[1]   Their

[1] "They which belong to the mystical Body of our

communion is a participation, growing ever more large and full, in the life of God's great family; it is a bond of union, a sacred kinship, binding them to one another and to God.

But who are thus bound? To whom can we properly apply the title of "saints"? In the language of to-day the word "saint" is applied to one who is conspicuous above his fellow-Christians for the unusual holiness of his life, or to those who have departed this life leaving behind them a reputation for uncommon sanctity. Saintliness is thus regarded as a rare quality, and the title of saint is denied to the great mass of those who are trying to live Christian lives. But in the Bible we find the word used in a

Saviour Christ, and be in number as the stars of heaven, divided successively by reason of their mortal condition into many generations, are notwithstanding coupled every one to Christ their Head, and all unto every particular person amongst themselves, inasmuch as the same Spirit which anointed the blessed soul of our Saviour Christ, doth so formalize, unite, and actuate His whole race, as if both He and they were so many limbs compacted into one body, by being quickened all with one and the same soul."
—Hooker, *Ecclesiastical Polity*, V. lvi. 11.

much larger sense. In the Old Testament
all those who were in covenant with God
were commonly described as saints. Every
loyal Jew was by his acknowledgment of
that covenant *separated* from the Gentile
world and devoted to the service of God.
He might not be living a faultless moral
life, but as a member of God's "holy nation,"
His "peculiar people," the Scriptures spoke
of him as a saint. In the New Testament
it is much the same. All who have been
brought by baptism into covenant with God
are addressed as "saints." When St. Paul
writes letters to the Churches which he has
established in the faith, he gives their
members the general title of saints. He
does not mean to imply that they are all
living holy lives, for in the very same letters
he rebukes them for the indulgence of grievous
sins. But he writes to them all as saints, *i.e*
baptized followers of Christ.[1]

[1] "There are two words in the Old and New Testament,
as they were originally written, which are expressed in the
English version by the one word-'saints': the one which
means properly holy, pure, and high, and separate from all

In apostolic and early Christian times the word was commonly used in the same generous way. It is only in later years that its application has been narrowed down to include only those who are remarkable for great purity of life and strength of character. To a careful student of Holy Writ and the Church's best literature, the popular use of things else; and this is the word which is applied to the most high nature of Almighty God Himself, as when the cherubim and seraphim cry to one another, 'Holy, holy, holy, is the Lord of Hosts.' Whereas the other word seems to bring with it the thought of tender and especial affection too. It is the word applied to the Incarnate Son of God, when it is said, 'Thou shalt not suffer Thine Holy One to see corruption;' and from Him the title is derived and flows, as it were, down to His blessed ones on earth. One of the two words, then, seems to refer to the glorious yet awful privileges of all, whom God has chosen to be a people to Himself, the other to the especial love with which He regards such as make a right use of those privileges. Accordingly the word 'saints,' which in our English answers to both these, has two somewhat distinct meanings: sometimes it stands for all Christians, all whom God's Holy Spirit has marked and taken out of the world to be Christ's own, sometimes for those who in an especial manner have laid hold of that glorious privilege, clung to it, brought it home to themselves, lived and died in the constant endeavour to get the perfect victory over sin, and live as nearly as they might the life of the very angels on earth."—John Keble, *Sermon on the Glory of the Saints.*

the word seems unwise and unwarranted. It
narrows what the Holy Spirit of inspiration
has left broad. It obscures one of the most
important features of Christian life and
character. It darkens the counsel of God
and shuts out some of the light of truth
which He has given us. The framers of our
creed used the word in a broader and more
scriptural and truer sense.[1]   They meant

[1] "This part of the article beareth something of a later
date than any of the rest, but yet it is no way inferior to the
other in relation to the certainty of the truth thereof. And
the late admission of it into the creed will be thus far
advantageous, that thereby we may be the better assured of
the true intent of it, as it is placed in the creed. For it will
be in no way fit to give any other explication of those words
as the sense of the creed than what was then understood by
the Church of God when they were first inserted.

"Such persons, then, as are called by a holy calling
and not disobedient to it; such as are endued with a holy
faith and purified thereby; such as are sanctified by the
Holy Spirit of God and by virtue thereof do lead a holy life,
'perfecting holiness in the fear of the Lord;' such persons,
I say, as are really and truly saints; and being of the Church
of Christ (as all such now must of necessity be), are the
proper subject of this part of the article, the Communion of
Saints, as it is added to the former, the Holy Catholic
Church."—*Bishop Pearson on the Creed.*

The English Reformers gave their interpretation of this
article of the creed in the *Institution of a Christian Man*,

it to include all souls, whether living on earth or in Paradise, who have been sanctified in the waters of baptism and are true to their baptismal covenant. They did not restrict it to those who have passed out of this life, nor to the possessors of peculiar sanctity. They gave it freely to all who were in covenant with God. Their use of it rests upon solid ground. Man is not the judge of sanctity. God alone can search out the ground of the heart. He alone " knows what is in man." How shall we dare to say that this man shall be called a saint and that other beside him shall not? We may be utterly deceived. It is well that the Church in her corporate capacity should recommend to her children certain apostolic and early saints of Christ for our reverent imitation ;

set forth by the authority of the bishops in 1537. " It is to be noted that, although the lively members of the Militant Church be subject to the infirmities of their flesh, and fall ofttimes into error and sin ; yet they always in Scripture be called holy, as well because they be sanctified in the blood of Christ, and professing in their baptism to believe in God and to forsake the devil and all his works, they be consecrated and dedicated to Christ."

and we gladly and with profit to our souls keep the days on which she commemorates their model lives. But if she, or any man or men, should attempt to draw a sharp line of distinction between the followers of Christ, and label those on one side of it as " saints," and those on the other as sinners striving to become saints, she will commit a grievous and presumptuous sin. Christ and His ancient Church drew no such line. In Scripture and in fact every loyal follower of Christ is a saint.[1] What is it that makes a saint ? It is this—consecration of one's life to Christ. That is what we mean by sanctity—separation from that which may defile a man, dedication of ourselves to God. The sign of a saint is not miracles ; it is not munificent works of philanthropy ; it is not great accomplishments for Christ and His

[1] " The mark of a saint is not perfection, but consecration. A saint is not a man without faults, but a man who has given himself without reserve to God. In the language of the New Testament, every baptized Christian—dead, and buried, and raised with Christ—is a saint."—Bishop Westcott, *Social Aspects of Christianity.*

Church. These may be the fruits of sanctity, but the thing itself is deeper and better than they. It is something which God alone can unerringly see and estimate.[1] I claim the name of saint for every soul that has been baptized into Christ and tries to live up to its baptismal vows. I claim it for every life that can with any degree of truth be called a consecrated life. I claim it for every one (however frail, however full of faults) who yet looks longingly before where Christ has gone and tries to follow Him. And who shall dare to deny my claim? Let such an one beware how he would deprive the humbler followers of Christ of their rightful share in the comfort and consolation and strength to be found in the fellowship of the saints. The spiritual life has no aristocracy, with vested rights and exclusive privileges.

---

[1] " We, whose eyes are too dim to behold the inward man, must leave the secret judgment of every servant to his own Lord, accounting and using all men as brethren both near and dear unto us, supposing Christ to love them tenderly, so as they keep the profession of the gospel, and join in the outward communion of saints."—Hooker, *Sermon V.* 11.

Its blessings and its benefits are free to every
child of God. Every Christian may claim
them for himself. The title and privileges of
sainthood are not a distant thing to which we
cannot attain. *They belong to us. We are
saints. You and I are saints.* We are trying
—are we not?—to serve and follow Christ.
Then we need not be afraid to claim our
rights by virtue of relationship to Him. We
shall do injustice to ourselves, unless we
remember that we are among the saints of
God and have our share in their communion
and fellowship. "We are numbered with the
children of God, and our lot is among the
saints" (Wisd. v. 4).

We have now defined our terms and can
go deeper into our subject. We are ready
to ask, What is the communion of saints?
What is it that they share with one another?
What are the relationships by which they are
bound? We shall find that these questions
involve a great deal, and stretch away into
realms of life and thought which perhaps we
have never explored. It will take some time

to answer them. But let us here take a brief glance over the field and mark out the boundaries of our course. Let us go hastily over the ground.

The saints have communion first with God in His triune personality. They are bound to Him by a relationship which nothing can break. They are children of God, members of the great Family of Christ, partakers of the divine life. Every one of them, even the humblest and most wayward, is in this sweet and sacred relationship. We are not as those who know not God. His love and mercy go out to them, I know, and they may perhaps be saved and we may yet be lost. But still our position is different from theirs. At our baptism we were adopted into the great Family of God, made members of Christ, and inheritors of the kingdom of heaven. We are therefore bound close to God in all the affectionate intimacies of a family life. He has admitted us into the inner circle, into the very heart of His life. We have our family secrets, our interior life, our sacred reserves,

into which the world dare not and cannot
intrude. Those who live outside our family
cannot know, they could not understand, all
that goes on within the sacred enclosure of
our life that is "hid with Christ in God."
They have never felt the sweet strong ties
that bind us to our Father-God. They do
not know what it is to have a Father and a
Home. Often we do not appreciate our
privileges, and sometimes we turn prodigal.
But that does not alter our relationship. We
are still sons, however prodigal and however
far from home. We are members of God's
household still, and the rich, warm life of
that household, with all its privileges and
possibilities, belongs to us. Our Father has
drawn us close to Him, taken us into the
most intimate of all relationships, and given
us a ground of confidence upon which only
children could stand. The highest enjoyment
of our family life is our loving intercourse
with Him. The hours that we spend alone
with Him are the sweetest of all hours. Our
family altar is the centre and source of that

life. There, apart from the world's noise and strife, we gather round the Table of our Lord. There our Father feeds us with the Bread of Life. There we bring all our childish plans and hopes and fears, and pour them into the great loving Father-heart. There we hear our Father's voice, and it speaks (oh, so lovingly!) straight into our listening hearts, warning, and comfort, and all such counsel as we need. There we feel the mighty tide of our Father's life, which pulses through all His human family. In its resistless flow it lifts us up out of ourselves, and carries us away, *where* God only knows. Oh, sweet communion and fellowship of the saints with God! Sweet and satisfying in the time of this mortal life, but in the life to come how far beyond all that we could ask or think!

If this were all, we might rest content. But it is not all. The saints on earth have communion with one another as well as with God. It is hardly less sweet than our fellowship with Him. In the Family of God we are bound to one another almost as strongly as to our

Head. The consciousness of our common life in the great household of God and of our mutual ministries about the house has power to sweeten and dignify every act of life. We are all working, each in his own appointed place and way, for the honour and welfare of our family. We hold the same faith. We join in the same hallowed words of prayer and praise. We have all the same aim. If one member of our family suffer, we all suffer with him. If one member be honoured, we ought all to rejoice.[1] There are few truths which have such power to strengthen and comfort us as this of the communion of the saints on earth.

There is one truth, however, which seems to me to have a wider and greater power than even this. It is the communion of the saints in light. It is a truth often neglected and obscured, but of fundamental importance in all true views of life. The Church of God is not all militant. Its vast majority has gone before, into the other life, and is now

[1] I Cor. xii. 26, 27 ; Col. ii. 19.

expectant. The number of God's saints on earth at any time is small compared with those in Paradise. These two grand divisions of Christ's Church, though their life is very different, are by no means separate. They are united in one communion and fellowship. They share the life of the one great Family of God. The saints in Paradise have passed beyond us and gone up into the higher stages of that life. But their relationship to us who remain behind is not broken in any real sense.[1] They are travelling the same road as we, only they have gone on before.[2] They

[1] "If I have communion with a saint of God, as such, while he liveth here, I must still have communion with him when he is departed hence; because the foundation of that communion cannot be removed by death. The mystical union between Christ and His Church, the spiritual conjunction of the members to their Head, is the true foundation of communion which one member hath with another, all the members living and increasing by the same influence which they receive from Him. But death, which is nothing else but the separation of the soul from the body, maketh no separation in the mystical union, no breach of the spiritual conjunction; and consequently there must continue the same communion, because there remaineth the same foundation." —*Bishop Pearson on the Creed.*

[2] "What a thing will it be, my brethren, what a joy and

C

are partakers of the same divine life as we,
only they have more of it. They have the
same faith and hope which they had on
earth. They are not unmindful of us and
of our life here. They wish us well. They
pray for us. Their prayers go up with ours
before God's throne. In God's sight and in
all true relationships they are at one with
us. Death cannot cut short our communion
with them.[1] They think of us, and love us,

what a wonder, when we shall come not only to believe and
hope, but to feel and know, that they have been all along
joining with us ! I say to you then, my brethren, practise
this faith : try to think of the holy ones departed as fellow-
travellers got on a little before us to the end of a journey
which they and you are making in common."—John Keble,
Sermon on the Communion of Saints.

[1] "As He is united with the Father, not by mere unity of
likeness or love or will, but by a true participation of His
Father's nature, 'God of God, Light of Light, very God of
very God;' so are we united with Him, not by any mere
unity of likeness, love, or will, but by a true participation
of His divine humanity. And as we are united with Him,
so with each other ; not by mere moral affinity or intellectual
agreement, nor by mere likeness of character or harmony of
disposition ; not by any outward figurative union which
changes communion into a play of imagination or a metaphor
of unsubstantial notions. The members of Christ's body,
both in heaven and earth, are united in a kindred as real as

and pray for us, even as we do for them. The seen and the unseen worlds are much closer than we think. They touch at every point. There is a vital union and communion between the two.

> "Angels and living saints and dead
>   But one communion make."

This doctrine of the communion of living and departed saints is what I wish chiefly to set before you in this book. It is the doctrine which was intended to be taught by the makers of our creed. It is a matter of record, a fact of history, that this is the sense in which they understood the words which they added to its ninth article.[1] They believed in the communion of saints as a mystical fellowship between all living and

the bonds of blood, but higher than all earthly brotherhood, by a participation of one common nature, of a restored humanity, sinless and deathless, in the person of the Second Adam."—H. E. Manning, *Sermon on the Communion of Saints.*

[1] "This is that part of the communion of saints which those of the ancients especially insisted upon who first took notice of it in the creed."—*Bishop Pearson on the Creed.*

departed saints.   They loved to think of
those who had entered into the unseen as at
one with themselves in all the realities of life.
They grasped the grand ideal of the great
Family of God with its unity of life on earth
and in Paradise.   In this primitive and
scriptural sense they believed in the communion of all the saints of God.   This
inspiring and satisfying belief is what I wish
to deepen in you.   I would open your eyes
and help you to see the bonds that bind this
to the other world, and realize the rich strong
life that fills them both.

Let us think for a moment of the unity of
the people of God.   We often sing of them
as an army.

> " Like a mighty army
>   Moves the Church of God ;
> Brothers, we are treading
>   Where the saints have trod ;
> We are not divided,
>   All one body we,
> One in hope and doctrine,
>   One in charity."

Oh mighty army of the living God!   I
seem to hear its solemn, ceaseless tread.   I

seem to see it passing by. I see children in the ranks. Like youthful crusaders of old time, they march beneath the standard of the Cross. I see the new recruits. Proudly and bravely they join the army of the Lord. I look further on to those who have been longer in the fight. I see the veterans. Their ranks are thinned, and many a vacant place tells its pathetic tale of wayside falls and battles fierce and long. Those who are left bear many a sign of conflict. Many a wound and scar tell of the hard-fought fight. But oh! their faces, how they shine with high resolve and the sweet sense of victory almost won. I see the battle-flags. Some of them are bright and fair, and from their crimson folds "the Cross shines forth in mystic glow;" but some are worn and tattered now. They have been rolled in dust and blood. I would not have them other than they are. I hear the voices of the men. Some are singing songs of victory, and some of the great deeds they think to do for God. But some are silent now. They have no heart to sing.

Their thin ranks and the tears on their cheeks
tell why. Onward and ever on the mighty
army moves. It seems to have no end. I
look from company to company to see if I
may find an end. I see a wall of darkness,
a pillar of cloud, which overhangs a valley,
deep and dark, through which all seem to
pass. I look away to the sunny highlands
which stretch beyond the valley where the
shadows lie, and there, behold, a still more
mighty host that marches the same heaven-
ward way. The conflict past, they make their
triumphal progress to the city of their King.
Their Captain goes before, the victorious
Leader of the whole lengthening host. Every
soul, on this side of the veil and on that,
acknowledges his leadership. Those who
follow closest after Him, do they forget those
who are still behind, who are still in the thick
of the fight? No, they love to hear how it
goes with them, and long for the time when
they too shall enter into light. And those
whose warfare is not finished yet, who have
not entered in behind the veil, do they not

often think of those gone on before?[1] Are they not conscious of the long array that stretches onward and upward to the throne of God? Though no voice comes back to them across that hollow vale, do not those silent columns beckon and draw them ever on? Does it not give courage and strength to think of the victorious ranks that stretch before? Surely it is so. The army of our God is one. It follows one great Captain who is gone before. It marches under one standard, the Cross of Christ. It has one aim and one reward, the crown of everlasting

[1] "In 1859, after Magenta, a vast army marched through a country thickly covered with shrubs and small trees. As the soldiers plodded wearily on, none could see more than a few hundred comrades on the right or left. Then at last a vast open plain was reached, where, instead of marching, corps after corps, they were deployed across the plain simultaneously in line of battle. The setting sun gleamed on miles of arms and glittering standards, and the eye of every soldier flashed and his cheek flushed at the magnificence of the spectacle. They were really as strong and as close before, but each fraction had a depressing sense of isolation. They now became aware of their strength: the next day was Solferino. Such courage is given to the soldier of Christ by the visible unity of the Church to which he belongs."—The Bishop of Derry.

life. Throughout its length, in all its parts it is the one army of the living God.

> "One the light of God's own presence
> O'er His ransomed people shed,
> Chasing far the gloom and terror,
> Brightening all the path we tread.

> "One the object of our journey,
> One the faith that never tires,
> One the earnest looking forward,
> One the hope that God inspires.

> "One the strain that lips of thousands
> Lift as from the heart of one;
> One the conflict, one the peril,
> One the march in God begun.

> "One the gladness of rejoicing
> On the far eternal shore,
> Where the one Almighty Father
> Reigns in love for evermore." [1]

[1] *Hymns Ancient and Modern*, 274.

CHAPTER II.

IS THERE A LIFE AFTER DEATH?

"THEY which say that the souls of such as depart hence do sleep, being without all sense, feeling, or perceiving, until the Day of Judgment, or affirm that the souls die with the bodies, and at the last day will be raised up with the same, do utterly dissent from the right belief declared to us in Holy Scripture."

These are the words of the fortieth Article of Religion adopted by the Church of England in the year 1553. They give the answer of the Church of their day to that irrepressible question, Is there a life beyond the grave? Upon the answer to that question we must be agreed before we can gain a full belief in the Communion of Saints.

The thing which we call death is a separation of what God has joined together. He

has made man a trinity, binding together in
one personality a body, a soul, and a spirit.[1]
Disease, the consequence of original sin, has
power to break this bond. It can separate
the body from the spirit and the soul. So
long as they are bound in one, this mortal
life goes on. The moment their union is
broken by disease or violence, it comes to an
end. But what then becomes of the members
of the human trinity ? The body is laid in
the grave. The soul and spirit, whose continued union we tacitly acknowledge by
speaking of them familiarly as the soul, what
becomes of them ?

[1] See Gen. ii. 7 and 1 Thess. v. 22. Of this second
text Bishop Ellicott says, in his sermon on the *Threefold
Nature of Man:* " From the days of Irenæus down to our
own, this text has been confidently appealed to as an
emphatic statement of the elements and constituents of the
nature of man. Though amidst much diversity of interpretation, and much variety of exegetical detail, it has still ever
been regarded by thoughtful men as a distinct and almost
formal exposition of the mysterious economy of our being ;
it has been deemed a most authoritative statement of the
triplicity in unity of human nature, and a witness that may
not be gainsaid of the existence and association of three
elements in man—body, soul, and spirit."

We are confronted by three alternatives. Is the soul annihilated and reduced to nothingness? Does it pass into a sleep in which it is as good as dead? Or has it an unbroken life beyond the grave? These are deep questions, which have always exercised men's minds, and to which we must earnestly address ourselves.

First, is the soul annihilated at death? Some have thought that death means the absolute destruction of both body and soul, and that neither of them can ever live again. Others have held that the soul is annihilated at death and ceases to exist, but is brought back to life or recreated at the judgment-day. But all such ideas are opposed to the general judgment of mankind, the teaching of the Christian Church, and the doctrine of God as declared in Holy Writ. There is an instinct in every soul which says that it is made for immortality. No course of reasoning will ever silence the cry of the human soul for life. The instinct is deep and ineradicable. Its presence indicates that God has made the

soul to live and not to die.[1]   Science has
never proved that a soul can die.   In fact, the
whole tendency of science seems to be the
other way.   It has established the indestructi-
bility of matter, has taught us that not one
single atom in all God's universe can be lost
or go to waste.[2]   It has thus proved the im-

[1]   " ' *Non omnis moriar* (I shall not all die)' is a consciousness of my rational nature.   It clings to me at every moment.
It is confirmed by my hopes and by my fears, by the dictates
of my reason and by the instincts of my heart, by my conscious
relation to a Supreme Law-giver, by my whole sense of
moral responsibility to Him, and by a sleepless anticipation
of an account, a balancing, and a completion hereafter of my
moral life and state now.   And this consciousness is not derived from sense, nor dependent upon sense.   I am more sure
of its truth than of any reports of sense and of any syllogisms
of logic.   Moreover, what I find in my own consciousness I
find to exist in the consciousness of others ; and not of one
or two here and there, but of all about me.   And I read of
it as having existed in all men, at all times and in all places.
And this *communis sensus* of men is a certain evidence of
truth, not so much by reason of the multitude of witnesses,
as by the universal voice of human nature, which is the voice
of its Maker and its Judge."—Cardinal Manning, *Meta-
physical Society's Papers*, No. 65, p. 7.

[2]   The following quotations will show with what confidence
scientific men have come to speak upon this point : "In all
cases where matter disappears—as in the burning of wood
or the evaporation of water—the vanished matter has only
undergone a molecular change which renders it temporarily

mortality of the soul. Shall I believe that
God who economizes atoms will squander
souls? Must I think that a soul, a life, created
in the image of God, has a less valuation than
a clod or a grain of sand? Why should life
be less permanent than matter, or why should
it depend upon matter for its permanence?
Cut off my arm ; you do not touch my life,
you do not curtail the powers of my soul.
Amputate or paralyze all my limbs ; my life
goes on, it is as true and large as it was
before. And when at last you reach my
vital organs, and reduce my body to a breathless motionless mass, what ground have you
to think that my soul is dead?[1] How do

imperceptible by our unaided senses." "It is now incon-
ceivable that a particle of matter shall either come into
existence or lapse into non-existence."—Prof. John Fiske,
Cosmical Philosophy, i. 281, 65.

[1] "Our organs of sense and our limbs are certainly instruments which the living persons, ourselves, make use of to
perceive and move with : there is not any probability that
they are any more ; nor, consequently that we have any other
kind of relation to them than what we may have to any other
foreign matter formed into instruments of perception and
motion, suppose into a microscope or a staff, nor consequently
is there any probability that the alienation or dissolution of

you know that you can kill my soul? You
cannot destroy one atom of my body. You
cannot prevent it from forming new combi-
nations and filling some new place in God's
material universe. Well, then, if you cannot destroy matter, how shall you destroy
soul? You may separate matter from some
soul to which it has been joined, and force
the soul to fill some new place in God's
spiritual kingdom, as the atoms do in the
material world. But you cannot touch the
soul; you cannot hurt or harm it; you
cannot kill it. It is immortal, it cannot
die.[1] As a part of God's created universe it
must be so. There *must* be a life beyond

these instruments is the destruction of the perceiving or
moving agent."—Butler's *Analogy*, i. sect. 2.

[1] "Just as Jesus' personality is in His divine nature, so
man's personality is in his spiritual nature. As Jesus is God
tabernacling in human nature, so man is a spirit tabernacling
in an animal nature. Now death cannot lay its hand on the
spirit and cause it to cease to be. It can exist under very
varied conditions in a body smitten by sin, or in a glorified
body, or out of the body; it can exist in Paradise, or in
Heaven, or in Hell. But one thing it cannot do—it cannot
pass into non-being." — Canon Body, *The Revelation of
Paradise*. (See St, Matt. x. 28-31.)

the grave. Am I to think that this life, with its vast inequalities of pain and happiness, is all? Is there no hereafter, where the patient bearers of life's burdens, the heroic sufferers of pain and injustice and self-sacrifice, shall find their reward? Dives has received his good things in his lifetime here on earth and Lazarus his evil things (St. Luke xvi. 25). Is there nothing for Lazarus in a life to come? The eternal justice of God demands that he have a future life, and in that life—we may not doubt it—God will satisfy his soul. " I know that my Redeemer liveth," and while He lives no soul can die. He has a human soul which He has united to His divine personality. Therefore I am partaker of His eternal life. My life is in vital connection with His unfailing life. No power can annihilate my soul. My real life, the higher, inner, truer life, my personality, my *self*, is beyond the reach of harm. It cannot die. It is as eternal as God Himself.

But does not the soul sleep in the intermediate state? Granted that it is indestructible and that in some sense it may be said to live, is not the life one of unconscious repose? This question is not new, and there are no doubt many to-day who would answer it in the affirmative.[1] They claim to rest their belief largely on the Old Testament. They find death spoken of often in its pages as a sleep, and they draw the conclusion that at death the soul enters upon a state of unconsciousness. But a careful study of the places

[1] The idea of a "soul-sleep" was maintained by the *Thnetopsychitæ* in the third century and opposed by Origen. It was revived in Arabia in the Middle Ages, receiving (as it was supposed) the approval of Pope John XXII. Later on it was held by the Anabaptists, against whom Calvin wrote his "Psychopannychia," and in a more moderate form by Luther and the Arminians and Socinians. It was condemned in the Councils of Florence and Trent. In more modern times it has been taken up by the Irvingites, and has found advocates in the English Church, as the following quotations will show :—

"The soul remains in a state of profound sleep, of utter unconsciousness, during the whole interval between its separation from the body at death and its reunion at the resurrection."—Archbishop Whately on *The Future State.*

"The next act in the history of the believer after he has closed his eyes in death is opening them in resurrection to receive the reward of victory. All between is a blank."—Rev. R. Courtenay, *Future States.*

to which they refer shows that the Scripture writers were speaking of the body rather than the soul. When they spoke of the dead as sleeping with their fathers, as sleeping in the dust, they referred to the repose of the body in the grave and were not thinking of the soul.

But we find in the Old Testament Scriptures stronger expressions than these. What shall we say of them? The psalmist makes this bitter cry: "Shall Thy lovingkindness be declared in the grave? or Thy faithfulness in destruction? shall Thy wonders be known in the dark? and Thy righteousness in the land of forgetfulness?" (Ps. lxxxviii. 10–12). The melancholy writer of Ecclesiastes takes a still darker view: "The dead know not anything, neither have they any more a reward; for the memory of them is forgotten. Also their love, and their hatred, and their envy, is now perished; neither have they any more a portion for ever in anything that is done under the sun. . . . There is no work, nor device, nor knowledge, nor wisdom, in

D

the grave, whither thou goest " (Eccles. ix. 5,
6, 10). What shall we say to such sentiments
as these enshrined in Holy Writ ? The
answer is one which in our study of the
Bible we ought always to bear in mind. The
revelation of God has not been given to the
world all at once. It has been progressive
and cumulative. Beginning far back in the
world's history, the light of God's Word has
very gradually shone through the gross
darkness which covered the people. It was
not until the close of our Lord's earthly life,
and not even then, that the full light of the
gospel shed its bright beams over human
life. When, therefore, we read the Old
Testament, we must expect to find some
things left dark or only dimly revealed. We
must wait for the fuller light which came with
the coming of our Lord. Especially is this
true of the Old Testament references to the
life after death. When they were written our
blessed Lord had not yet "brought life and
immortality to light." We must expect to
find in the Old Testament imperfect and

gloomy views of death. We must correct them by the brighter and more hopeful teachings of the Lord, and we must remember that they were spoken of the body rather than of the soul.

There is one further scriptural phrase which claims our attention. Our Lord, just before He raised them from the dead, spoke of Lazarus and Jairus' daughter as "sleeping." Did He mean that their souls were asleep? As this question will be answered indirectly later on, I think it will be enough for the present to say that our Lord was speaking simply of the repose of the body in death and that He used this expression to emphasize the wonderful "awakening" of that body which they were just about to witness in each case. His definite teaching (as I shall try to show later on) contradicts the idea that He spoke of a sleep of the soul.

This whole question of the sleep of the soul after death seems to me a very plain one. I know of no evidence that the soul can sleep. Science has never told us so. On the contrary, it has many wonderful things to tell us about the action of the mind while the body is asleep. Scientists and philosophers of the highest eminence have maintained that the mind never sleeps, that its activity goes on unceasingly during what we call sleep.[1] They say that what we call dreams are simply fragments which we have happened to remember out of the constant processes of thought which went on in our sleep. If, therefore, we gave the fullest credence to those who speak of death as a sleep, we do not thus imply a slumber of the soul. Just as during bodily

[1] The continual energy of the intellect was maintained by Plato and Cicero, as well as by St. Augustine, *De Anima et ejus Origine.* "Just as the heart never ceases to beat, but sends its pulses throughout every vein, so the mind never ceases to busy itself in some form of thought." "The mind is always thinking," was one of the favourite sayings of Des Cartes, who held that "if he should cease wholly to think, he would cease wholly at the same time to exist." Kant claims that we always dream when asleep, and that to cease to dream would be to cease to live ; also that we dream more in a minute than we can act in a day, and that the great rapidity of thought in sleep is the chief cause why we do not recollect all we dream.—*Anthropology*, § 30. Substantially the same views have been held by Leibnitz, Jouffroy, Sir William Hamilton, and many more modern philosophers.

sleep the mind is awake and active, so in the sleep of death we should not hold that the soul is paralyzed into inactivity. But we are not bound by such expressions, except so far as the body is concerned. In the absence of any scientific proof that the soul can sleep, and in the presence of weighty scriptural evidence to the contrary, we affirm that the condition of the soul after death is not one of sleep.

It now remains for us to consider the third alternative which we have set before ourselves, and our hearts will turn to it with the keenest interest. There is a natural inclination of the human heart to believe in a life beyond the grave. The heart follows its vanished kindred out of this life into the beyond, and refuses to believe that they have ceased to be. We could bear to be separated from them for a time, but not to think that they have gone out into nothingness. And the same is true of every good and saintly life. We instinctively resent the thought that any life full of high qualities can be destroyed and brought

to nought.   We feel it a moral contradiction
that such a life, a Christ-like life, should come
to a sudden and an utter end.   We believe
in a true " survival of the fittest."   We feel
with St. Peter that it "was not possible"
that such a life "should be holden" of death
(Acts ii. 24).   The question, therefore, Do the
departed souls live a personal individual life?
will be one of absorbing interest.

We have already answered it indirectly by
showing that they are not annihilated and do
not sleep.   But there is direct and positive
evidence to the same effect, and that evidence
comes mostly from the lips of our Lord.   In
the parable of Dives and Lazarus (St. Luke
xvi. 19–31) He gives what we are bound to
recognize as in its essential underlying principles a true picture of the life of the unseen
world as it was then.   We cannot with any
show of reverence think that our Lord used
the language of the day, knowing it to be
inaccurate, simply to give a vivid colouring
to His parable.   There must have been some
existing realities which the parable was in-

tended truthfully to represent. I would not insist too much on the minute details into which the parable runs, but upon the underlying truth, which the whole was intended to convey, *I do insist.* The truth to which I refer is this, that, whatever changes it may bring about, death does not break, nor even temporarily interrupt, the individual personal life of any soul. The parable pictures the life of this world as carried on without a break into the unseen. Lazarus is Lazarus still. Dives is Dives still. Death has not destroyed nor changed their personality. Abraham is there and is Abraham still. They speak to one another as living beings, having a separate personality. In this parable, then, spoken under the most solemn circumstances, when He Himself was looking death in the face, our Lord seems to teach us that human personality reaches into the life beyond the grave, that the individuality of souls is not lost in the other world. Surely this is the essence of the truth which the parable was intended to teach. If it does not teach that

the lives of Dives and Lazarus were uninter-
rupted by death, in the name of God what
does it teach, and what is it worth?

But we are not left to parables alone.
Our Lord gives us other weighty words.
He speaks from the cross, to the penitent
thief, in the very hour of death. He promises
him, "To-day shalt thou be with Me in Paradise" (St. Luke xxiii. 43). This promise implies the continuance of two personalities after
death. It ought to satisfy every reasonable
mind. No human words could surpass these
in clearness and positiveness of assertion.
"To-day *thou* shalt be with *Me.*" Not thy
body with Mine in the grave. Not thy spirit
with Mine in Paradise. But *thou* with *Me*,
thyself with *Myself.* Thou who hast sinned,
and suffered, and repented on the cross, with
thy Saviour who hangs beside thee here.
Thou shalt enjoy with Me a companionship
which shall be living, genuine, sweet, and
satisfying to thy soul. No meaning short of
this would have brought comfort to that
broken and contrite heart, or been worthy

of the loving Lord who spoke the words. Unless there was to be real life, and he who received the promise was to be in some true sense himself and able to enjoy the presence of his Lord, what was the promise worth to him? But the words of Christ were not empty words. They were chosen with divine fore-thought and intelligence. They were full, yes, infinitely full, of truth and life. His promise to the thief must mean the unbroken identity of being on both sides of the veil. As St. Ambrose loved to say, "Where the Lord is, there is life."

To sum up what has been said, what I have to teach is this: the existence of a continuous personal life which death has no power to break. On the contrary, death makes it larger and freer than before. It strikes off the fleshly fetters with which it has been bound, and sets the soul free. It removes that life out of all the earthly surroundings which clog and corrupt it here, and lifts it up into a purer atmosphere. Death is a new birth into a higher, larger

life. To every saint of God it is the opening
of a vast horizon that stretches even up to
heaven's gates, and is all radiant with the
smile of God. Why is it that we keep the
day of a martyr's death rather than of his
birth into this world? Did you ever think
why? When the Church tells us to keep
a holy day in memory of St. Stephen or
St. Mark, she does not choose the day of his
natural birth into this world; she takes the
date of his death, of his martyrdom. And
why? Because that is his true birthday, the
day of his birth into the Paradise of God,
the beginning of his real life. On that day
it was that his soul, set free from all that
chained it here on earth, began to truly
live. "Put to death in the flesh, but quickened in the spirit."

This doctrine of the individual, indestructible personal existence of every human
soul is a most precious belief. It glorifies
God and it comforts men. It claims un-
dying life for every departed soul. It dries
the tears from every eye, and wipes them

away from all cheeks.   The souls that we
have loved, the holy lives that we have
reverenced, they are not at an end.   They
have not ceased to be.   Death cannot
destroy those souls, those lives; hell cannot
do it; God will not do it.   They are " alive
for evermore."

CHAPTER III.

WHERE ARE THE SOULS OF DEPARTED SAINTS?

THERE is an inquiry which springs up naturally out of every human heart. Many a time we have asked it of ourselves, of God, and still the selfsame question echoes through our thoughts. Where are the saints who have been withdrawn from our sight? They have gone from us, and we know that their places here on earth will be vacant till the end of time. We believe that they have not gone out into nothingness, are not wrapped in a dull unbroken slumber, nor lost in oblivion. But where are they, the true and holy ones whom we have loved and reverenced? Are they in darkness or in light? In earth, or heaven, or hell? Where is their place and what their part in God's wide universe? Are they far from us or near? Where is their abode, and what their life between the hour of death and the judgment-day?

These questions are right and natural; they cannot be repressed. We must answer them as best we can. We cannot answer them so fully as we would. No one has come back from the unseen world to tell us all that we would know. There was a time when, round an open grave at Bethany, there gathered close an awestruck, silent throng and listened for such words. They saw Lazarus come forth from his charnel-cave. But he brought with him none of the secrets of the other world. Though he continued with them probably for thirty years, and often and again they must have tried to draw from him the story of his life beyond the grave, he found no words to tell it in. They were left to guess from the calm face, so full of awe, that never smiled again, the secrets of that life behind the veil.[1]

[1] There was an apocryphal writing ascribed to Lazarus, which narrates his experience of the unseen world, three

> " ' Where wert thou, brother, those four days ? '
>   There lives no record of reply,
>   Which telling what it is to die
> Had surely added praise to praise.
>
> " From every house the neighbours met,
>   The streets were filled with joyful sound,
>   A solemn gladness even crowned
> The purple brows of Olivet.
>
> " Behold a man raised up by Christ !
>   The rest remaineth unrevealed ;
>   He told it not ; or something sealed
> The lips of that Evangelist." [1]

God has not permitted those who have
been called back from the other world to
tell us of its life.   In fact, it was not possible.

books of which were supposed to have been hidden by the
apostles, and the fourth carried to Rome.   Some of the
apocryphal gospels pretend to reveal something of the other
world, but they are valuable only as indicating the tradi-
tions and beliefs of early Christian times.   The traditional
story of the after-life of Lazarus tells us that his first question
as he came forth from the tomb was whether he should die
again, and that, being assured that he was still subject to
the common doom of men, he was never seen to smile again.
Epiphanius represents him as having survived for thirty
years, and tradition makes him the first bishop of Marseilles,
martyred and buried there.

[1] Tennyson, *In Memoriam* xxxi.

It cannot be told to human minds in human words.[1]   The life beyond the grave can never be fully comprehended till we find ourselves in its midst.   There are, however, some things about it which we can know even now.   A careful reverent study of God's Word will tell us much—as much as we are able now to grasp.   Let us try by its help to answer our question, Where are the souls of departed saints ?

Do they go at once to their final abode ? The popular theology of the Protestant world answers that they do.   In its violent recoil from the monstrous claims and manifold superstitions with which the doctrine of purgatory had become involved, it rushed madly into an opposite extreme.   It blindly declared that those who die in the Lord are translated at once into the full enjoyment of the heavenly life, and that those who have lost their souls enter without delay upon a

[1] We have this upon the authority of St. Paul, who tells us that when he was caught up into Paradise he heard "unspeakable words, which it is not lawful for a man to utter" (2 Cor. xii. 3, 4).

life of utter separation from God.[1] It is
difficult to understand how any logical
thinker or conscientious student of Holy
Writ could have taken such ground. The
New Testament, and especially the teaching
of our Lord, is absolutely fatal to any such
belief. That teaching, given in most unmistakable terms, amounts to this : that there
will be a great judgment-day at the end of
the world ; that on that day the bodies of all
mankind shall be raised from the sleep of
death and reunited to their souls ; that they
shall be publicly judged for the deeds done
in the body ; that then, and not till then,

---

[1] " Puritan eschatology may be described in the language
of art as a ' study in two colours,' and those the blackest and
the whitest. There was no gradation; there was neither
warmth nor tenderness such as one sees in nature everywhere,
in the blended softness and brilliancy, smoothness and bold-
ness, light and shade of earth and sky and sea. The whole
thing was as bare and bald and decided as a New England
country meeting-house. There was heaven and there was
hell, and the line between them was terribly abrupt and
sharp. Some souls went at once to one, and others went
just as promptly to the other, and the reason for this sudden
and inexorable fixedness in good or bad, eternal woe or
eternal bliss, was not quite evident to human reason."—Rev.
Walker Gwynne, *Some Purposes of Paradise*, p. 12.

shall they enter on their heavenly life. That
life is everywhere revealed to us as one in
which the body as well as the soul shall have
its part. It was so with our Lord Himself.
His humanity did not enter on the heavenly
life till after He had risen from the dead.
Even on His resurrection-day He warned an
impetuous worshipper, "Touch Me not; for
I am not yet ascended to My Father" (St.
John xx. 17). It was forty days after His
resurrection, and forty-three days after His
death upon the cross, before He began
His heavenly life as the Son of Man. And
just so, the Scriptures teach us, every human
soul must wait until its body has been raised
from the grave, and God's general [1] judgment
passed before it can enter on its final state.

[1] I do not ignore the *particular judgment* which Catholic
theology teaches us is passed upon every soul in the hour of
death, and which fixes its eternal destiny. ("It is appointed
unto men once to die, but after this—a judgment," Heb.
ix. 27). The final public judgment of mankind, when all
the results of our conduct as well as the deeds themselves
can be brought to light, and the justice of God in His dealings with the human race be vindicated, is, however, made
so prominent in Scripture as almost to eclipse the thought of
an individual judgment at death.

E

When the great Baptist preacher, Charles
Spurgeon, died, the following bulletin was
posted on the Tabernacle doors: "Our
beloved pastor entered heaven at nine o'clock
this morning." But surely there was no
warrant for such words. I would not deny
one crumb of comfort to those who mourned
his loss, nor would I put a stigma on his
earnest life. All honour to that life, all credit
to his faithful work for God! But still the
facts remain. God's great day has not yet
come. The throne of judgment has not been
set. Charles Spurgeon's body rests in the
grave, and will rest there so long as this earth
shall last. Till God shall raise it from the
dead, we have no right to think of him as in
the heavenly mansion which we trust is
being prepared for him. To do so would be
to put ourselves into flat contradiction with
the teaching of God's Holy Word as to the
resurrection and the heavenly life.

We come back, then, to our question, What
becomes of the soul at the time of death?
If it does not at once enter on the eternal life

of joy or woe, if it must wait till it is joined
to the body again and God's sentence has
been publicly pronounced, what of the inter-
vening years? From the hour of death to
the day of judgment may be a long waiting-
time. Is there an intermediate state in which
the spirit lives and waits the coming of God's
own good time? Our Church, our Creed, and
our Bible tell us that there is. The Church
in all ages, especially her earliest, has believed
in such a state of life. The Church militant
has always claimed relationship to the Church
expectant, the waiting Church, which so far
outnumbers her.[1] The Apostles' Creed declares
that after His death on the cross our Lord
"descended into Hell," which expression the
American Prayer-book interprets as meaning,

[1] In her Articles and in the teaching of her best divines the
Anglican Church since Reformation times has plainly taught
the existence of an intermediate state. It would be easy to
fill such a volume as this with quotations from a multitude
of her best doctors, but it may be enough to mention that
such men as Bishops Jeremy Taylor, Pearson, Bull,
Andrewes, Horsley, Butler, Forbes, and Browne in England,
and Bishops Seabury, White, Wainwright, and Hobart in
America, have taught it as a *de fide* doctrine of the Church.

" He went into the place of departed spirits,"
where they wait the coming of the last great
day.   The word " Hell " is used in the creed
in a scriptural sense somewhat different from
that which it has in the ordinary language of
to-day.   It does not mean there the final
abode of the lost, although Calvin understood it so.   That place is expressed in
Scripture by the word " Gehenna."   The creed
uses the word " Hell" in the sense of " Hades,"
which was understood by the Jews to be a
waiting-place for departed souls.   Into that
place it assures us that the spirit of our Lord,
like every human soul, went to await its
resurrection-day.   As used in the creed, the
word " Hell" carries with it no necessary idea
of torment or suffering.   It does not intend
to suggest the monstrous thought that our
Lord endured the sufferings of the lost.   It
simply tells us that His human soul went the
way of all souls.

The Holy Scriptures teach us distinctly,
though somewhat indirectly, of the existence
and character of the intermediate state.

First they insist with great emphasis on the
resurrection and final judgment as preparatory to the entrance of man into his eternal
heritage of gain or loss.   Our blessed Lord
most positively declared that "no man hath
ascended up to heaven but He that came
down from heaven, even the Son of man
which is in heaven" (St. John iii. 13).   Later
on He spoke of Himself as about to go, on
the day of His death, into a place which He
called Paradise.   He did not mean heaven,
for He did not go there until forty-three days
had passed.   On the morning of His resurrection He said of Himself, " I am not yet
ascended to My Father" (St. John xx. 17).
By Paradise He must have meant some
intermediate state preparatory to the heavenly
life into which He was later on to ascend.
Speaking of the resurrection, St. Paul says
that those who are then "alive and remain
shall be caught up together with them in the
clouds, to meet the Lord in the air " (1 Thess.
iv. 17).   "Together with them," *i.e.* with all
those who have died in faith and are some-

where waiting for the second coming of their
Lord. The Epistle to the Hebrews, after
enumerating the saints of the old covenant
and their virtues, reminds us that, although
they died in faith, they have not yet received
the fulfilment of God's promises, but are
compelled to wait in an incompleted state,
"that they without us should not be made
perfect" (Heb. xi. 40). Finally, when the veil
was lifted and St. John looked into the unseen
world, he saw the souls of the Jewish martyrs,
not yet admitted to heaven, but waiting under
the altar and crying out, "How long, O
Lord, holy and true, dost Thou not judge and
avenge our blood on them that dwell on the
earth?" The answer to their cry is, "Rest
yet a season, until your fellow-servants also
and their brethren . . . be fulfilled" (Rev.
vi. 10, 11). And before the great Seer saw
"a new heaven and a new earth," he "saw a
great white throne," he "saw the dead small
and great stand before God, and death and
hell" (*i.e.* hades, the underworld) "delivered
up the dead which were in them, and they were

judged every man according to their works "
(Rev. xx. 11, 12, 13). Then at last he saw
"the holy city, New Jerusalem, coming down
from God out of heaven," and the multitudes
of them that were saved began to walk in
its light.

The existence of some state of life for
disembodied souls seems distinctly enough
declared in the Holy Scriptures. But do
they tell us anything about that life, where
it is, what its surroundings, conditions, and
possibilities are? Yes, they do. Not so
fully and explicitly as we might desire, but
they give us many hints which will help us
to understand (so far as it is best for us to
know) the interior life of the spirit-world.
Let us take up some of the descriptive
phrases which we find applied to the intermediate state, and see how far they will
furnish an answer to our question, Where are
the souls of departed saints?

We have already heard the martyrs spoken
of by St. John as "waiting under the altar "
(Rev. vi. 9) until the course of their fellow-

servants should be fulfilled. In all times the
altar of God has been regarded as a place
of refuge, a sanctuary from the violence of
men, a calm and safe retreat. So when
the souls of the martyrs are described as
"under the altar," it is meant that they are
in the safe-keeping of God; that He has
hidden them from the strife of tongues and
the provoking of all men, and is treasuring
them up in His storehouse against the time
to come.[1] We find, therefore, the saints of
the old covenant pictured as withdrawn
into a safe retreat, under some restraint, and
longing for the time when their number
should be made complete, and the "white
robe" of the righteousness of the new covenant should be given them.[2]

The next description of the departed saints
comes to us from St. Peter. He tells us that
our Lord, leaving His body on the cross,

---

[1] "Thou shalt hide them privily by Thine own presence
from the provoking of all men: Thou shalt keep them
secretly in Thy tabernacle from the strife of tongues"
(Ps. xxxi. 22).

[2] See Milligan, *Book of the Revelation*, pp. 97–103.

"went and preached to the spirits in prison"
(1 Pet. iii. 19). The idea here is not
necessarily that of penal confinement. By
the prison is meant a place of custody or
security. Bishop Horsley has defined it as
a "place of seclusion from the outer world,
a place of unfinished happiness, consisting of
rest, security, and hope, more than of enjoyment." Into this secure retreat, called by
St. Peter a prison-house, the human soul of
our Lord entered, and proclaimed there, as
well as on earth, the gospel of the kingdom
to those whom He found "in the passionate
yearning of expectancy and the pain of
unsatisfied desire."

The parable of Dives and Lazarus (St.
Luke xvi. 19–31) furnishes us with some of
the most prominent and important features
of our Lord's teaching on the intermediate
state. We find in it a most vivid picture of
the life of the other world, to which we shall
have to refer again and again. We shall not
attempt to exhaust its meaning here, but
will simply glance at the picture which it

presents. It shows us Lazarus at his death being carried into a place described as "Abraham's bosom." Dives, the rich man, after death, finds himself also in the place of departed spirits, in sight of Lazarus, but with an impassable gulf between, which makes it impossible to gain relief from him. The description of Lazarus as "in Abraham's bosom" was one which would carry a perfectly clear impression to the mind of every Jew. The highest Jewish ideal of blessedness was fellowship with Abraham in the covenant of God. He was the chief of the patriarchs, the friend of God, and nearness to him meant closeness to God. This figure of speech expressed the most intimate fellowship. Its image was borrowed from the festive customs of the time, in accordance with which the Jews reclined rather than sat at table, and rested their heads each in his neighbour's lap or on his breast. To be in "Abraham's bosom," therefore, was to share with him in the most intimate, affectionate intercourse the enjoyments of his life in the other world. The parable pictures Dives, the representative of the other part of the underworld, in a condition of unhappy expectancy. He realizes the folly of his worldly life, and seems to be filled with a sense of the irrevocable loss of his God-given opportunities. He is anxious to warn others, while there is yet time, to avoid his unhappy fate. While Lazarus is comforted, he is tormented by a fearful anticipation of the just judgment of God.

The conclusions to be drawn from this parable seem to me to be partly these : that the life of the soul goes on after death in some place or state provided by God for disembodied souls ; that this has two divisions or states of life widely separated from each other, at least in the tenor of their existence. In one of them the spirits of the saints (represented by Lazarus) enjoy rest, refreshment, and companionship. In the other, those who have squandered their lives and hardened their hearts to the extent of final impenitence, await with apprehension the just and final

judgment of their God. Their retribution
has begun. This intermediate state, in both
its parts, is mentioned in Scripture as Hades,
in our Creed as Hell.

Thus far we have been occupied with the
intermediate state as it was under the old
covenant. We have found it described as a
place of rest and security, but its inhabitants
(the saints of the old dispensation) hampered,
limited, confined in some way until the victory
of Christ should be complete, and they should
attain to the glorious liberty of the sons of
God, and gain that better thing which without
us they could not have.[1] "With Christ a new
morning dawned upon the realm of the dead.
As death has lost its sting through Christ, the
kingdom of the dead has lost its horrors for
those who believe in him."[2] The victory of
Christ over death, and His triumph and
passage through the intermediate state, must

[1] Rom. viii. 21 ; Heb. xi. 40.

[2] "Hebraism speaks of the state in Hades with a certain
terror, and associates a joyous and consoling expectation with
the hope only of the coming of the Messiah to earth."—Bishop
Martensen, *Christian Dogmatics*, 461.

needs have brightened what the old Fathers
regarded as at best a place of gloom, and
made the life beyond the grave a different
thing.[1] Accordingly we may expect to find
coincident with our Lord's entrance into the
other world a new and more hopeful view of
the future life.

There remains one further Scripture phrase
to be examined, and it also comes from the
lips of our Lord. On the eve of His entrance
into the unseen world, He speaks from the
cross to the penitent thief, "To-day shalt
thou be with Me in Paradise." By the word
"Paradise," as we have already seen, He did
not mean heaven. The time for His ascension had not come. He evidently intended
to describe some place of preparation for the
heavenly life. The word which He chose was
a familiar one. The Jews believed in an
intermediate state, and had come to speak

[1] This was a favourite thought in the early ages of the
Church, was taught by the Fathers, embodied in apocryphal books (see the *Gospel of Nicodemus*), and made the
theme of those mediæval mysteries which represented the
Harrowing of Hell.

of it as Paradise.[1]   The term was commonly
applied in the East to a royal park or pleasure-
ground, well wooded and watered, its slopes
decked with flowers, and the whole adapted
to the refreshment of those who journeyed
through deserts and dwelt under a sultry sun.
Its still waters, its cloistral shaded avenues,
its leafy coverts, where the sun never shone,
seemed to an Oriental mind the ideal of earthly
peace and quietness, the fit surroundings for
the palace of a king. This word our Lord
used, and ever since it has been a consecrated
word, and has been understood to mean the
outer court of heaven, the gardens of delight
which stretch about the dwelling-place of God,
the pleasant land in which all faithful souls
shall dwell until they enter in through the
everlasting doors into the palace of the Great
King. Its beauty must be transcendent, its

[1] Since the close of the Old Testament canon there had
grown up a broad popular belief, blending with the best
hopes of the Jews, of which the Second Book of Esdras
(especially the fragment of it recovered in 1875) gives us a
glimpse, to which our Lord appeals, and which He raises
to a new dignity, and makes it descriptive of spiritual
realities which before did not exist.

delights infinite. It must be worthy of that city of God which it surrounds, worthy to be the royal road that leads up to gates of pearl and into streets of gold.

There is one more thought. Our Lord's promise to the thief on the cross was not simply, "Thou shalt be in Paradise," but "Thou shalt be *with Me* in Paradise." That is the best thing we know about the inter-mediate state, and it is enough for us to know. To enter it is to be with Christ in some true and real sense, to draw closer to Him than we have been before.[1]   The Chris-

---

[1] "True, the Sun of Righteousness is in heaven, but He causes His light-giving, warming, fructifying beams to shine with wondrous power on those who are in His garden. He is in heaven, yet ever does He draw near to His own with whispers of His voice and ministries of His hand, as He reveals himself to His own through the Spirit. And, indeed, this spiritual nearness meets every need of a disembodied spirit. It could not see Him with a material eye; it can only see Him with the eyes of the understanding. It can but be near Him with a spiritual contact—that is, with a contact of mind and heart and will. But so sensible is this nearness that it is intended as a presence ; so clear this grasp of Jesus that it is indeed a vision. For in them knowledge is so wondrous a sight that the faithful in Paradise see Jesus with their whole being."—Canon Body, *The Revelation of Paradise.*

tian does not speak of being "in Abraham's
bosom;" he goes at death "to be with Christ,
which is far better" (Phil. i. 23).   He knows
that to be "at home in the body" is to be
"absent from the Lord" (2 Cor. vi. 8).   The
Lord is his Shepherd; he shall not want.   He
maketh him to lie down in green pastures;
He leadeth him beside still waters; He
restoreth his soul.[1]   In the nearer presence
of his Lord, under the shining of an eternal
light, he waits the coming of the perfect
day.

Our answer, then, to the question, Where
are the souls of departed saints? is this.   They
have entered a new, a higher sphere of life,
which differs totally from this material sphere
of time and space; "an inward realm where

---

[1] "As the twenty-second psalm gives us our Lord's prayers
and bitter sorrows during the hours of the Passion, as He was
passing through the deep waters of the dark river of death;
and as the twenty-fourth psalm describes the glory of Christ's
ascension; so the twenty-third psalm is as it were the hymn
of praise which He sang, when His disembodied spirit was
passing into Paradise."—Bellett, *The Dead in Christ*,
p. 47.

Its imagery, like that of Ezek. xxxi. 1-9, seems plainly
drawn from a royal Oriental paradise.

life lays bare its root, whereas in this world it shows only the branches of the tree;" "a kingdom of calm thought and self-fathoming, a kingdom of remembrance in the full sense of the word;" where the soul "draws itself back into the innermost and mystical chambers of existence," "resorts to that which is the very foundation of its life;" "a cloister-like conventual world;"[1] "a solemn hush of being, in which it is the part of the mightiest spirits to lie still."[2] They are spending "a school-time of contemplation," as in this world they endured "a discipline of service."[3] They dwell in "a peaceful expectation-land,"[4] a realm of progressive development. They are in a sure resting-place, a safe and holy treasure-house of God. They have entered "the ante-chamber of heaven, where souls may pause awhile before the King comes out to bring them into His secret presence-chamber, His supreme delights."[5] They are in the Paradise of God—

[1] Bishop Martensen.   [2] Bishop Woodford.
[3] Dr. Newman,   [4] Dr. Pusey.   [5] Mr. Gwynne.

F

> "The happy land
> Where they that loved are blest,
> Where loyal hearts and true
> Stand ever in the light,
> All rapture through and through,
> In God's most holy sight."

Finally, they are "with Christ," "at home with the Lord." In a close *unio mystica* with Him, in His safe keeping and sweet society, they wait the coming of the Great Day of God. "The souls of the righteous are in the hand of God, there shall no torment touch them. In the sight of the unwise they seemed to die, and their departure is taken for misery, and their going from us to be utter destruction: but they are *in peace.* For though they perished in the sight of men, yet is their hope full of immortality" (Wisd. iii. 1–4). "The hope of the ungodly is like dust that is blown away with the wind; like a thin froth that is driven away with the storm; like as the smoke which is dispersed here and there with a tempest, and passeth away as the remembrance of a guest that tarrieth

but a day. But the righteous live for
evermore ; their reward also is with the
Lord, and the care of them is with the Most
High " (Wisd. v. 14, 15).

CHAPTER IV.

DO THE SAINTS DEPARTED LIVE A CONSCIOUS LIFE?

Is the life of the soul in the Intermediate State a conscious life? This question opens up to us some of the most inviting fields of inquiry which can be traversed by the human mind. It sums up within itself some of the most fervent hopes and fears and longings which are felt by human hearts. Its width and depth are well-nigh infinite. We cannot answer it in full. Some of our deepest and most anxious questionings will bring us no response. We must not seek to be wise above that which is written, nor to pry too deeply into the things which are not seen. But, on the other hand, we ought not to know less than God would have us know. We need not fear to come close up to the bounds which He has set, beyond which we

may not pass. As the Beloved Disciple
stooped down and looked into the empty
sepulchre from which angel-hands had rolled
away the stone, so when God for a moment
draws aside the veil which hides the unseen
world, we need not turn away our eyes. We
may reverently look and learn.

Before we enter into the heart of our subject, there is one matter which it seems to me
we ought to settle once for all. We have
had occasion several times to refer to our
Lord's story of Dives and Lazarus, and we
shall make it the basis of further teaching
throughout the work. It is important, therefore, to determine how far it is " profitable for
doctrine." In our use of this parable we are
not restrained by the canon of interpretation
long ago laid down,[1] that parables are not
to be made primary sources of doctrine.
With the lesson which it was intended to
teach we are not directly concerned. We
have to do simply with the form in which

---

[1] By Irenæus, *Contra Hæresias*, ii. 27 ; Tertullian, *De
Pudicitia*, 8, 9 ; St. Anselm, *Cur Deus Homo?* i. 4.

our Lord chose to convey His truth. Desiring
to teach some definite lesson in a parabolic
form, He made use of certain imagery, gave
us what purports to be an illustration from
real life. Whatever doctrines we may base
upon this parable rest, not upon the teaching
which it was intended to convey, but upon
the genuineness of the materials with which
the Great Teacher clothed His truth. However we may differ in the interpretation of
our Lord's parables, we must agree upon this,
that their imagery is true to life. When the
Divine Limner undertakes to paint a back-
ground which is to be the setting of some
sublime and eternal truth, we may rely upon
the purity of His materials and the perfection
of His art. Our Lord's parables differ from
those of men notably in this—their inimitable,
often pathetic accuracy. Every one of them
conforms exactly to our experience of human
life. The Sower, the Good Shepherd, the
Prodigal Son, the Good Samaritan, and all
the rest of them, how literally and admirably
true to life they are! Our Lord's parables

bear the stamp of truth in every line. All
their details may not be essential to the
purpose of the parable, they may or may not
be a part of the lesson to be taught, but their
simple truth and reality are undeniable. It
is a sound and solid principle for us to go
upon that our Lord's use of parabolic materials
is always in strict accordance with the laws
of nature and the facts of human life. A
critical study of His parables will show that
they are drawn straight from real life, and are
in their minutest particulars true to life. Now,
if the story of Dives and Lazarus is a parable
of our Lord, these things must be true of it.
The only right and reverent course for us is
to accept it as a true picture of the life beyond
the veil. As one of the most learned scholars
of modern times has beautifully said, our
Saviour, in this parable, "does more than
merely paint pictures upon the veil; He
removes it entirely, so far as we with our
present eyes are capable of beholding.[1]" He
gives us a view of the inner realities of life.

[1] Stier, *Reden Jesu*, vol. iv. p. 224.

There is no indication of anything uncommon, or unreal, or miraculous in His words. The two men's lives on earth are such as we often see. The picture of their lives after death was in almost perfect harmony with the best Jewish belief of our Lord's time. It is alluded to as if it were the natural and unvarying course of events. There is every reason to suppose that the hearers of the parable so accepted it, and understood our Lord as setting His seal upon the popular belief. It may be safely said that the Catholic Church has always regarded this parable as a true picture of the Intermediate State under the Old Covenant. It is, therefore, to be received by us as, in all its important particulars, a revelation of the life beyond the grave.[1]

We may now, having got our foundations solidly laid, proceed to erect the edifice of our belief. The question of a conscious life of the soul after death is one which has often exercised the Christian Church. Future

[1] See Appendix I., on "The Parable of Dives and Lazarus," p. 89.

consciousness has never been denied by any
large part of the Church or of the world.
Ancient literature is full of it, and the instincts of mankind have always pointed to it
unerringly. Some Stoic philosophers hushed
the heart-voices that clamoured for it and
awed them into a sullen silence. Some
theologians of the Middle Ages believed in
a slumber of the soul. Some people of to-
day think that the soul can die. But the
masses of mankind have had no sympathy
with such gloomy thoughts, and the Christian
Church, whenever she has spoken, has condemned them. She has always maintained
the unbroken consciousness of the soul's life.
When we turn to Holy Scripture, we find
nothing to indicate that death can suspend
or break the conscious existence of the soul.
As we have already seen, when the Old or
New Testament writers speak of the sleep
of death, they refer to the body, not to the
soul. Even though their words should be
applied to the soul, it is plain that the
gloomy forebodings of Old Testament saints

are not to be weighed against the authoritative utterances of our Lord. Our knowledge of these matters must be gained chiefly from Him. What has He to teach?

In His promise to the penitent thief upon the cross He distinctly asserts the continuance of consciousness. " To-day shalt thou be with Me in Paradise." Unless there was to be some real, conscious life, what was this promise worth? Can it possibly mean anything less than that? Is " unconscious slumber in a land of oblivion" equivalent to being with Christ? Surely our Lord's promise must have in it more meaning than that. It must imply that the soul is not shorn of its powers in Paradise.

Again, in the parable of Dives and Lazarus [1] we have a most vivid picture of conscious life. It is no torpor of soul, no dreamless sleep of the spiritual man, but a *life* full of hope and fear and desire. The consciousness of Dives is quickened, not dulled. He begs with an agony of desire that his five

[1] St. Luke xvi. 19-31.

brethren may be warned before it is too late. Abraham answers him, and they communicate with one another as reasonable beings. According to the methods of the spiritual world, whether in something analogous to human speech or not, they commune with one another across the gulf. Their souls are stirred by emotions somewhat the same as they felt in this life, and capable of being at least faintly shadowed forth in the language of this world.

Thus plain and clear is the testimony of our Lord. We might add much to the same effect from other portions of God's Word, but other questions claim our thoughts, and to every unprejudiced mind this must surely be enough.

Having, as I trust, established the fact of consciousness in the future life, we want to know what are its activities. With what is it occupied? How is it limited? What are the main directions in which it moves? Is it more or less active than before? These questions and many more throng in bewildering confusion through our minds, and we

must try to answer some of them. But there
are certain things which we must not forget.
At death soul and body separate, and the
soul begins to live alone. It no longer
receives its impressions through sensations
of the body. The pains and pleasures of
the body belong to the past. The mind acts,
but no longer through bodily media. The
result is a great quickening of the mental
and spiritual faculties. They are no longer
clogged and confused by carnal lusts, but act
with a freedom and force and scope impossible before. The intellectual and spiritual
life is unhindered now, and a magnificent
horizon opens before it in which it is free to
range. We who are in the body must not
expect to realize all that is before it. We
can only partly comprehend and dimly guess
at its unseen activities. We must confess
our inability to understand the *processes* of
soul-life in the other world, and acknowledge
the limitations of our human faculties. But
whatever *has* been revealed and *is* comprehensible we must learn and profit by.

Now, so far as we are able to comprehend them, what are the occupations of the life beyond the grave? With what are souls busy in the unseen world? I answer, they are undergoing a process of soul-growth and ripening, a progressive sanctification, a purification from the defilements of this world. The vast majority of Christians, when they die, are in a very imperfect state. They are not fit for the heavenly life. The pure light of that holy land would bring into startling prominence the stains which this evil world has left upon their characters. Nor could they endure all at once the sight and near presence of their God. How shall they be prepared for their entrance into the life of heaven? In a moment? In the twinkling of an eye? By some sudden miraculous working of God's hand? Or by the quiet, steady operation of the Holy Ghost upon their ghosts in the spiritual world? The analogies of nature, where God works in slow well-ordered ways, would lead us to expect a slow progressive sanctification of the soul

after death. The Church, founding her belief
upon the Word of God, has always held this
latter view. She has limited the educative,
formative processes of soul-life, not by the
boundary-line of death, but at a point far
beyond—"the coming of our Lord Jesus
Christ." [1] She teaches that the life after

---

[1] See Phil. i. 6. "The point of death is rarely referred
to by our Lord or His Apostles. The great boundary-line
of man's life is always a point away beyond death, namely,
the Resurrection and Final Judgment. All life here on
earth, and in the bodiless condition in Paradise, is regarded
for Christians as one unbroken ascending plane, one connected whole. Death is not mentioned even once in our
Lord's great discourse concerning 'the last things.' The
climax in the parable of the Ten Virgins is the coming of
the bridegroom ; in that of the Talents, it is the return of
the lord ; in that of the Pounds, the return of the noble-
man. So, too, in the Marriage Feast it is the entrance of the
king ; in the wheatfield it is the harvest home ;—all signifying,
not death, but 'the end of the world' and the final judgment."—The Rev. W. Gwynne, *Some Purposes of Paradise*, 26.

" ' Perfection' and 'holiness' are high, almost unimagin-
able, attainments for mortal men, and the thought of this
alone would forbid us to limit such sayings to the close of
probation. But in no case can we fix that limit, for it is
remarkable and too often forgotten, that the *objective*, so to
speak, of the apostolic vision is not death, but the 'day of
the Lord.' It is true that the main direction of a soul *to
God* or *away from God* is fixed by its time of probation here

death is not an inactive life, but that in it
the souls of all saints are being gradually
transformed into the image of Christ.   In
the sunlight and warmth of His presence
they are growing, ripening, mellowing.
Upon some of them the beatific vision of
God may have already begun to dawn.   The
impurities of heart and life which hindered
them from seeing God are purged away.   The
prayer which the Church taught us to pray
for them as they went out from our midst
has been fulfilled.[1]   The scars of their old
sins have been effaced, the lingering love of

but it has been beautifully and truly said, that though the
tree may lie in the *direction* in which it falls, there is much
of shaping and carving for the Master-Carpenter to do upon
the tree before it is fitted to be a pillar in the heavenly
temple.   God's work of cleansing and completing, we may
then be sure, goes on in that mysterious land where 'they
rest from their labours,' where they are in preparation for
completed blessedness."—Canon Knox Little, *Sunlight and
Shadow in the Christian Life.*

[1] That "whatsoever defilements it may have contracted in
the midst of this miserable and naughty world, through the
lusts of the flesh, or the wiles of Satan, being purged and
done away, it may be presented pure and without spot before
Thee."—The Commendatory Prayer in the Office for the
Visitation of the Sick,

worldly things which while in the body they could never quite escape is gone, the last remnant of sinful passion has been "purged and done away," they are at last "made meet for the inheritance of the saints in light." [1]

But what are the individual activities of the soul in Paradise? Does it know the past? Does it know all mysteries? Does it know other souls? I think we can satisfy these deep questionings.

Does the soul in Paradise remember the past? We have substantial grounds for believing that it does. Those who have come back to us from the gates of death tell us that in the time when they hung between life and death, memory was wonderfully quickened. Their past life flashed before them with startling distinctness. This may have been the awakening of memory to the more vigorous activities of the unseen life. At any rate, our Lord seems to distinctly declare that there will be such quickened

[1] See Appendix II., on "The Doctrine of Purgatory," p. 94.

activity. In His parable (St. Luke xvi. 19-31) to which we have before referred, the first words of Abraham to Dives are, "Son, remember;" look back over the past and recall the course of God's dealings with you on earth. Dives had already remembered other things. He had thought with agony of his five brethren who were still in the flesh. He could not forget the danger which stared them in the face. Now he was to remember his own course of life.[1] But if

---

[1] "The kingdom of the dead is a kingdom of *remembrance* in the full sense of the word—in such a sense, I mean, that the soul now enters into its own inmost recesses, resorts to that which is the very foundation of life, the true substratum and source of all existence. Hence arises the purgatorial nature of this state. As long as man is in this present world he is in a kingdom of externals, wherein he can escape from self-contemplation and self-knowledge by the distractions of time, the noise and tumult of the world; but at death he enters upon a kingdom the opposite of this. The veil which this world of sense, with its varied and incessantly moving manifoldness, spreads with soothing and softening influence over the stern reality of life, and which man finds ready to his hand to hide what he does not wish to see,—this veil is torn asunder from before him at death, and his soul finds itself in a kingdom of pure realities. The manifold voices of this worldly life, which during this earthly life sounded together with the voices of eternity, grow dumb, and the

G

Dives could remember in the unseen world,
surely Lazarus could do the same.   Without
the contrast which memory would draw between the "evil things" which he had
suffered in his earthly life and the "good
things" which he now enjoyed, he would be
deprived of a large part of his reward.   How
sweet to him now to live over the past,
and compare his "light affliction, but for a
moment," with the "eternal weight of glory"
now in view!   Arguing from Lazarus and
Dives to other souls, I claim for them the
blessed activities of memory.   The scenes of
this world's life, the well-known haunts, the
old familiar faces,—they are not forgot.   In
thought, at least, the saints departed fondly
linger near the spots they loved on earth.
How much they know of our present life
we cannot tell with certainty.   But that they
remember us, and think of us, and cherish
their old love for us, we cannot doubt.   The

holy voice now sounds alone, no longer deadened by the
tumult of the world, and hence the realm of the dead
becomes a realm of judgment."—Bishop Martensen, *Christian Dogmatics*, 458.

pure and precious loves of this life are not forgotten in the life to come. God is love, and He will not quench any love that has a right to live. Our friends who have gone before love to muse over the lives we are living now. They love to think of the great struggling Church on earth, and to live over the battles they have fought in her ranks. And if there come thoughts of penitence and visions of past sins, as come they must, with them will come a fuller knowledge of the loving mercy of their Lord to soothe the self-accusing pangs of memory.[1]

[1] "Shall we think that we can remember Bethel, and Gibeon, and the Valley of Ajalon, and Jerusalem, and the Mount of Olives; but that Jacob, and Joshua, and David, and the Beloved Disciple, remember them not? Or shall the lifeless dust that their feet stood upon be remembered, and the living spirits who there dwelt with them be clean forgotten? Surely we may believe that they who live unto God, live in the unfolded sameness of personal identity, replenished with charity, and filled with a holy light; reaching backward in spirit into this world of warfare, and onward in blissful expectation to the day of Christ's coming: and in that holy waiting adore, as the brightness of Paradise ever waxes unto the perfect day, when the noontide of God's kingdom 'shall be as the light of seven days,' and shall stand for ever in a meridian splendour."—H. E. Manning, *The Sleep of the Faithful Departed.*

But are we right in speaking of fuller light
in Paradise? Yes, I think we are. The
path of the saints is not only a purgative
but an illuminative way. They have entered
into the shining of a perpetual light which
shineth more and more unto the perfect day.
That light must illuminate the mysteries of
life and make at least some of them plain.
They are "with Christ" in a nearer, truer
sense than before; surely closer contact with
Him must teach them much. They are
entirely submissive now to the will of God.
Shall not then the promise reach to them,
"Whosoever doeth the will of God shall
know of the Doctrine"? Dives in the place
of departed spirits took larger, truer views
of life; and shall the same be denied to the
saints in light? Shall God, who gave man
knowledge, hide it from him at the very
time when He is perfecting him for an
entrance into the very fulness of knowledge?
I trow not. What will be the limits of that
knowledge we may not dare to define; but
that in its gradual growth it will far surpass

the knowledge possible in this world we may
rest assured.

We must pass on now to our final question,
which is one of breathless interest.   Do souls
recognize each other in Paradise?   Do the
friendships and loves of this world continue
in the next?   I answer that, if they are pure
and true, they do, and I find solid foundations for this belief.   The voice of humanity
has always pleaded that it must be so, and,
being the universal outcry of the human heart,
we shall expect to find it confirmed by God,
the Maker of that heart.   We find it so confirmed in God's written Word.   Lazarus in
Paradise is described as being "in Abraham's
Bosom;" that is, in familiar affectionate intercourse with Abraham.   In the picture which
our Lord gives us of their life in the underworld they recognize one another.   Abraham
and Dives and Lazarus all identify each other.
The personality and the relationships which
they had on earth are regarded as unbroken
still.   They communicate with each other,
even across the gulf.   The loving care of

Dives for his brethren who are still on earth
endures beyond the grave. He pleads for
them with Abraham (St. Luke xvi. 27–30).
The whole story is based on the unmistakable
mutual recognition of these three souls in the
unseen life. Our conclusion is that, if three
know each other, then all may, and the
prophecy shall be fulfilled, "Many shall come
from the east and west, and sit down with
Abraham, and Isaac, and Jacob," in the enjoyment of conscious fellowship. The promise
of our Lord to the penitent thief upon the
cross is another important piece of evidence
to the same effect. It implies recognition in
Paradise, or else the promise is almost worthless and comfortless. Unless there was to be
some companionship and loving intercourse,
what would it profit him to be with his Lord
in Paradise? To deny him all power of
recognition after death would be to make
that gracious promise of none effect.

Such Scripture statements as these, uncon-
tradicted by human reason or by other parts
of God's Word, ought to satisfy us that there

will be full recognition in the future life.
There is a communion of saints in Paradise.
The " glorious company of the Apostles," the
" goodly fellowship of the Prophets," the
" noble army of Martyrs," are all united in that
sweet society. And every lesser saint, down
to the least, has his place and part in it. The
members of the great family of God are not
strangers there. The ties with which God
bound them or they bound themselves are
not dissolved nor broken now. They are only
purified, and uplifted, and made stronger
than before. The special loves which bound
them here on earth bind children and parents,
husbands and wives, pastors and people, there.
Ever-growing love for God neither weakens
nor replaces them. He has made these
earthly ties and encouraged us to make them,
that they may all be golden chains to bind
us to one another and to Him. He will not
cut them loose, but rather draw them closer
day by day. We may be sure that all true
friendships and all love which deserves to
live will survive the shock of death, and be

matured and perfected in the life of Paradise. It is an almost overwhelming thought. The associations and friendships of to-day—we are making them for eternity. If they are good, and true, and sweet, and pure, then such shall they be for evermore. If they are false, and base, and contaminating to the soul, we shall be dragged down and enchained by them everlastingly. For we shall carry on into the future life the associations which we form in this. As we go out of this life into the other the sentence will be pronounced, "He that is unjust, let him be unjust still ; and he which is filthy, let him be filthy still ; and he that is righteous, let him be righteous still ; and he that is holy, let him be holy still" (Rev. xxii. 11). O magnificent possibilities, intense realities, sublime dignity, eternal import of this human life !

APPENDIX I.

IT has generally been considered by the Church that when our Lord related this story He was making use of a true history. It would be easy to cite a multitude of eminent doctors who have so regarded it. Amongst the Fathers of the Church, Justin Martyr, Clement, Irenæus, Origen, Tertullian, Cyprian, Jerome, Epiphanius, Basil, Hilary, Chrysostom, Augustine (?) and Ambrose so received it, and they have had many followers in more modern times. Indeed, tradition has always pointed out the houses of Dives and Lazarus in the *Via Dolorosa*. But the historical character of the narrative is not essential to our purpose. Whether our Lord quoted a piece of actual history for illustrative purposes, whether His story was one of

fact or only founded on fact, is immaterial
to our inquiry. Of its verisimilitude we may
rest assured. "He who knows perfectly the
fitness of things and their correspondences
needs not to mix up the true and the false
for the purpose of teaching the true" (Pollock,
Out of the Body, 152). Our Lord, therefore,
is giving a true picture of Dives and Lazarus
on both sides of the grave.

But it must be remembered that in the
later part of the story He is picturing spiritual
realities which are largely incomprehensible to
human thought and inexpressible in human
words. It is almost impossible for us to
imagine an existence which is incorporeal,
and so the whole revelation of God has been
made comprehensible to men by the use
of anthropomorphic terms. Holy Scripture
speaks of the face, the arm, the hand, the
finger, of God, and thus accommodates itself
to our sensuous modes of thought. But we
know well enough that such terms are used
to describe (so far as it can be done in
human speech) that which is immaterial and

spiritual, and we do not fail to grasp the heavenly truths which were intended to be conveyed. Such language helps us to realize the powers and activities of God.

In the story of Dives and Lazarus we encounter the same modes of speech. Our Lord speaks of the bosom of Abraham, the eyes and tongue of Lazarus, and of torment in a flame such as we associate only with bodily suffering. But we know that the fleshly bodies of these three persons had been laid in the grave and were not risen yet, for Christ had not yet "brought life and immortality to light." We are warranted by the whole tenor of Holy Scripture in interpreting the language of the parable as a condescension to our finite intelligence, an attempt to convey in human speech (the only language in which God can make himself intelligible to man) such knowledge as is possible of the life of the unseen world. These are figurative modes of speech, and yet they express substantial spiritual realities. None of them is meaningless ; the truth is, they are charged with more meaning than they can convey. They are meant to teach us that the same processes of life which formerly manifested themselves through bodily media are still going on in the Unseen. Though very inadequate, they are the best descriptions which can be given us of the soul-life there. While they describe the other life in terms of this, use body-words to describe soul-life, they picture vividly and truly (if we will but understand) the activities of disembodied souls in the unseen spiritual world, and are to be received by us as revelations of existing realities.

Stier's treatment of this subject (*Reden Jesu*, vol. iv. 223–229) is most valuable. I quote Sadler's view, given in his *Gospel of St. Luke*.

"If it be asked how can a disembodied spirit feel bodily pain, or what is equivalent to it and must be described in the same language, we answer by asking the question, 'What is it within us which feels pain?' Evidently not the mere wounded fleshly muscle, but the animal life, the soul in fact, to and from which the nerves which permeate all parts of the body carry the sensations which the soul feels, for if the nerve which forms its link of communication with the stricken or burnt limb be severed or withered, the self or soul feels no pain. Just, then, as the soul can think independently of the brain, though the brain is in some way, unknown to us, the instrument in its act of thinking, so the soul may feel that which can only be described in terms which indicate bodily pleasure or pain, though it is apart from the body."

APPENDIX II.

THE DOCTRINE OF PURGATORY.

"As no soul leaves this present existence in a fully complete and prepared state, we must suppose that there is an intermediate state, a realm of progressive development, in which souls are prepared and matured for the final judgment. Though the Romish doctrine of Purgatory is repudiated because it is mixed up with so many crude and false positions, it nevertheless contains the truth that there must, in a purely spiritual sense, be a Purgatory designed for the purifying of the soul."

These are the words of the learned Lutheran Bishop Martensen (*Christian Dogmatics*, 457). They indicate very fairly the ground which is occupied by a large proportion of the non-Roman theologians of to-day, and which is not far from the Catholic Doctrine of the Church. The belief in a purgative discipline of the soul dates back to ante-Christian times. It was held in a more or less definite form by the Jews, and in some heathen writers (notably Virgil, *Æneid*, vi. 735-747) we find it set forth. While it is not directly taught in the New Testament, there are numerous passages which seem to fall in with such a belief (see St. Matt. v. 26; xi. 22-24; St. Mark ix. 49; St. Luke xii. 48; 1 Cor. iii. 13; Rev. xxi. 27). Even Dean Farrar has been forced to confess that in the doctrine as stated above there is nothing "in any way inconsistent with Scripture, while it certainly is consistent with a very ancient belief of the Church" (Preface to *Eternal Hope*). The Fathers of the early Church, when their writings are examined and compared, present to us a two-sided truth, whose opposite faces they are not always at pains to reconcile. They re-echo with great force and frequency the angelic declaration, "Blessed are the dead which die in the Lord." They speak with serene confidence of the great body of the faithful departed as being in

peace. But at the same time they speak
often and earnestly of " the benignant philan-
thropic fire " by which every man's work
shall be tried, using language which may be
well summed up in the words of Eusebius
Gallus, " Thou who⁻ hast done things worthy
of temporal punishment, to whom is addressed
the Word of God, 'that they go not out
thence until they pay the uttermost farthing,'
through the fiery stream, which the prophetic
spirit mentions. In proportion to the matter
of the sin, will be the lingering in the
passage ; in proportion to the growth of the
fault, will be the discipline of the discerning
flame ; in proportion to the things which
iniquity in its folly has wrought, will be the
severity of the wise punishment." It is in the
reconciliation of these contrary views that
the sum and substance of their teaching must
be found. The mediæval corruptions which
gathered about the belief in Purgatory as it
had before been held are well known. They
were both doctrinal and practical. The
doctrine of a treasury of merits accumulated

by Christ and His saints, transferable at the pleasure of the Pope to needy souls, and available for them in the Unseen World at the purchase of their friends on earth, so commercialized the practice of the Church, that (in words framed by one of modern times) she seemed to say, "Down with your cash, and as the money clinks in the box the soul that you care for is delivered from its pains." Her popular teachers materialized their descriptions of the purgative processes of the Unseen World down to the grossest possible form, coloured them with startling vividness, and then traded on the fears they had aroused. It was while this state of things was unreformed that the Church of England framed her twenty-second Article in which the Romish doctrine concerning purgatory and pardons was condemned as a " fond thing vainly invented, and grounded upon no warranty of Scripture, but rather repugnant to the word of God." That this condemnation was merited by the popular teaching and practice of the time no one can doubt. The

H

Church of Rome acknowledged as much
when she set herself to reform the abuses
against which such loud complaints had been
raised. But it cannot be held to have been
directed against the authoritative Roman
doctrine of to-day, nor still less against the
Catholic doctrine which comes to us from
earlier times. The Article was framed before
the Council of Trent had pronounced upon
the questions and abuses involved in it. It
therefore was intended to condemn, not the
Tridentine decrees which were formulated
afterwards, and which alone are of authority
in the Roman communion to-day, but the
current corrupt teaching and popular practices of the time. In this sense we unhesi-
tatingly subscribe to it, although those
abuses have since been largely reformed.
But in doing so we do not deny the existence
of a Purgatory rightly understood. We
simply fall back upon the purer and more
primitive belief which the early Church
held to be involved in the doctrine of the
Communion of Saints. We cut loose from

all the false theories and corrupt practices of
the mediæval Roman Church, but we cling
to the underlying Christian truth on which
they were a fungus growth. While we
stigmatize the gainful superstitions of the
past, and indignantly deny that "the gift of
God may be purchased with money," while
we repudiate the grossly materialized pictures
conjured up by the heated imaginations of
Jesuit preachers, we do reverently believe in
a progressive preparation of the soul after
death to enjoy the Beatific Vision of God.
"Without holiness no man shall see the
Lord." No vestige of sin must cleave to
the soul which is to stand before God. The
cleansing process, if not completed in this
life, must go on in the other world. Nor can
we think it capable of being carried on without conscious exertion and suffering there as
here, although the soul is so enkindled with
the desire of becoming at one with God, that
it gladly embraces and rejoices in any discipline which its good God may provide. It
is in peace, because its particular judgment is

past, and it is consciously progressing Godward. Its joy is deepened with every step
which brings it nearer Him. It would wish
us to pray, not so much that its discipline
may be abridged, as that God may work His
will in it to the uttermost. Its chief desire
is that everything may be consumed away
which would hinder God from flowing in
upon the soul. In the words of St. Catherine
of Genoa, "When the soul by interior illumi-
nation perceives that God is drawing it with
such loving ardour to Himself, straightway
there springs up within it a corresponding
fire of love for its most sweet Lord and God
which causes it wholly to melt away; it
sees in the Divine Light how considerately
and with what unfailing providence God is
ever leading it to its full perfection, and that
He does it all through pure love; it finds
itself stopped by sin, and unable to follow the
heavenly attraction,—I mean that look which
God casts on it to bring it into union with
Himself; and this sense of the grievousness
of being kept from beholding the Divine

Light, coupled with that instinctive longing which would fain be without hindrance to follow the enticing look, these two things, I say, make up the pains of the souls in Purgatory. Not that they think anything of their pains, however great they be; they think far more of the opposition they are making to the will of God, which they see clearly is burning intensely with pure love to them. God meanwhile goes on drawing the soul to Himself by His looks of love mightily, and, as it were, with undivided energy; this the soul knows well; and could it find another Purgatory greater than this by which it could sooner remove so great an obstacle, it would immediately plunge therein, impelled by that conforming look which is between God and the soul."

Thus we have the two sides of the old Patristic doctrine harmonized, and find ourselves upon solid ground, as believers in a gradual purification of the soul in Paradise from all the rust of sin until it is prepared to "see God."

CHAPTER V.

WHAT IS THE RELATIONSHIP OF DEPARTED SAINTS TO US?

IN the last three chapters we have been considering the state of the faithful departed. We have satisfied ourselves, I trust, that their life goes on uninterruptedly in Paradise with Christ; that it is an individual life, with an identity distinct from other souls; and that it is an active life, a progressive sanctification under the influence of the Holy Ghost, in which there is memory of the past, increased knowledge of many things, and conscious intercourse with other spirits in the Unseen. The three following chapters will be somewhat larger in their scope, and will treat of the relationships which practically constitute the Communion of Saints. First, we are to think of the relations which the faithful departed sustain to us. It is important for us to know how and how far their lives in Paradise influence us, if at all.

The first question which confronts us is this: How much do they know of our present life and needs? Are all the events of the world's history and of our individual experience known to them? This question involves important issues, and ought to be answered cautiously.

One testimony of Scripture will instantly suggest itself. The writer to the Hebrews, after setting in array the saints of the Old Covenant, and recounting the triumphs of their faith, addresses his readers in stirring words which suggest the contests of the amphitheatre: "Seeing we also are compassed about with so great a crowd of witnesses, let us lay aside every weight, and the sin which doth so easily beset us, and let us run with patience the race which is set before us" (Heb. xii. 1). But when we examine the passage in the original Greek, we find that the writer deliberately avoided the use of several familiar words for "spectators," and chose another not at all synonymous with them, namely, μαρτύρων, "witnesses," the same word which we use for those who have laid down their lives in defence of the faith. The natural interpretation would be that we are surrounded by a great company of martyrs (in will, if not in deed), who have witnessed to God's truth, and whom we ought to imitate. Whether they are spectators of our struggles in the same cause, the passage does not clearly reveal.[1] It would, therefore, be somewhat rash to claim it as evidence that the departed know all that is passing in the world which they have left.

When we ask ourselves whether there are any inherent powers by which disembodied souls must necessarily be conscious of passing human events, we find none. Their

---

[1] Such has been the judgment of the ancient Fathers in general, and of many of the best modern divines. See Alford and Vaughan on the Hebrews, and Dean Luckock, *Intermediate State*, 246-249. Other passages of Scripture which bear upon the subject will be noticed later on.

memory of the past involves no minute acquaintance with present worldly affairs. Their gradual growth in knowledge in Paradise relates rather to the things of God than to the things of men. God is educating them up to the Judgment Day, but the knowledge of all that goes on here might be rather a hindrance than a help to His educative processes. It might distract the soul from higher pursuits. They live a changed life. It is natural to think that they are now isolated from, cloistered away from, the restless activities of this workday world, and not by any immediate power of apprehension conscious of what goes on in it.[1]

Let me put this before you in another's words, which are better than any which I can command. He says, " I can only think with solid satisfaction of the present state of

---

[1] Such passages as Isa. lxiii. 16, 1 Kings viii. 39, 2 Kings xxii. 20, seem to fall in with this. We find no warrant either in Scripture or patristic writings for the Roman teaching that the saints who have entered into the beatific vision from the nature of their blessedness see all human affairs as in a mirror of the Godhead.

the blessed dead as removed away from, and
above, the interests of earth, and perfecting
holiness in the brightness of Christ's presence.
It would bring me no consolation to conceive
of them as borne, like clouds, somewhere
between earth and heaven, with affections
divided between both. It might sometimes
bring momentary pleasure to think that some
deep sorrow was being shared by them, as
of old, or some unwonted joy; but surely,
brethren, there would be a selfishness in the
thought; their 'white robe' might be almost
sullied, their blissful waiting troubled, by such
participation. No; their present life is in
another sphere of being altogether. When
they put off the earthly tabernacle at God's
call, they laid aside, for a time at any rate,
the thousand interests which had gathered
round it. Their love for, their memory of,
us whom they have left centres rather in our
inward and invisible, than in our outward and
seen, life. I venture to think that they would
not, if they could, follow in thought the ups
and downs of our present daily life, taking

part, as they then must needs be doing, by sympathy at least, in our petty vexations or refreshments, or even our well-doing or our weaknesses. They regard us now, if I may so express myself, more as they regard themselves, in reference to the large, broad, absorbing question of our fitness for the coming presence of the great God and Saviour. They realize now what He meant when He spoke, as He so often did, of losing life to find it. They have found *their* life, and their one predominant concern is whether we are finding *ours*. We may not wish it otherwise. Our work for a while, a *little* while, must be done alone, so far as regards their knowledge of what we do." [1] We may wisely accept the general tenor of these words, and hold with St. Augustine that for the departed to have an inherent and minute consciousness of human affairs is impossible. But there is a counter truth which we must not ignore. While they do not know by their own

[1] The Rev. Canon Swayne, *The Blessed Dead in Paradise*, 36.

powers of perception what passes here, such
knowledge may be conveyed to them through
other avenues.   Their numbers are increasing
day by day, and each soul that goes hence
carries with it into the other world some
news from this.   The angels, as they go to
and fro upon their ministries from God to
men, let fall by the way so much as God
permits them to tell of what is going on
here.   Finally, our Lord Himself imparts
to the souls which dwell in His nearer
presence something, as much as it is best
for them to know, of what is happening to
those whom they have loved and left behind.
Thus, while we have no proof that they know
of themselves all that is passing here, we are
at liberty to think that their loving Lord lets
them have such knowledge of us as they need.
It may not be complete, it may not go into
particulars, but it is enough.[1]

[1] Samuel's knowledge after death of the wickedness of
Saul and the calamity which was to follow it (1 Sam.
xxviii. 15–21), Moses' and Elijah's knowledge of our Lord
and "His decease which He should accomplish at Jerusalem" (St. Luke ix. 30, 31), and Abraham's knowledge

We may now take up another question which no doubt lies very near our hearts.

of the earthly lives of Dives and Lazarus, and of the writings of Moses and the Prophets (St. Luke xvi. 25–31), are to be explained on such grounds as these, not as direct perceptions of their own. St. Augustine bestowed more thought upon this subject than any of the ancient Fathers. Commenting upon the Lazarus parable, he says of Dives' request for his brethren that "it does not follow that because the rich man said this, he knew what his brethren were doing or what they were suffering at that time. Just in the same way had he a care for the living, albeit what they were doing he wist not at all, as we have care for the dead, albeit what they do we confessedly wot not. For if we cared not for the dead, we should not, as we do, supplicate God on their behalf."—*De Cura pro Mortuis*, 17. Of Abraham's knowledge he says, "Not while the things were doing in their lifetime, but after their death, he learned these things by information of Lazarus." His conclusion of the whole matter is that, while the dead cannot by their own nature know what we are doing or suffering, something of it may be revealed to them. "It must be confessed that the dead are not acquainted with what is being done here, that is at the time when it is being done, but afterwards they hear from those who by dying go from hence to them; not indeed everything, but so much as those are permitted to declare who are suffered to remember them, and as it is meet for those to hear whom they inform of the same. The dead may also hear somewhat from the angels, who are present at the things done here, as much as He to whom all things are subject judges that any one of them ought to hear. . . . The spirits of the dead may also learn some of the things which are done here, and which it is necessary that they should know, through the revelation of the Spirit of God."—*Ibid.* 18.

What we have said thus far leads up to it.
Do the saints in Paradise pray? Do they
pray for us? And are their prayers effectual
for our good? They are now removed out of
the turmoil of this life and are at rest. But
they have needs. Therefore they must pray
to God. Death cannot silence the voice of
prayer. It cannot cut the soul off from God,
so that it cannot speak to Him. On the contrary, it removes one of our greatest hindrances
to communion with Him, that is, our flesh.
The souls in Paradise are with Christ, in a
closer fellowship than was possible on earth.
Their speech with Him must, therefore, be
freer than it was before. It must be frequent,
frank, and unrestrained. But when on earth
they prayed much for us. Our needs formed
the burden of their unselfish prayers. Have
they forgotten us and ceased to pray for us
now? Do they no longer plead for us with
God? Their needs are less and they have
more time for prayer. Has death struck
dumb the voice of intercessory prayer?
Unnatural and unchristian thought! The

souls in Paradise are still the same souls. They have not lost their identity. Their traits of character and their affections are the same as before, only exalted and purified. All that was good in them remains unchanged, except for the better. They love us still, they think of us, they long for the time when we shall join them in their holy home. Therefore they *must pray for us.* They must often and earnestly ask God to work His will in us and bring us safe home to them. They must plead with Him to protect us from harm and pardon all our sins. They do not need to be spurred on by a full knowledge of all that is happening to us. Out of their own experience they can guess our needs well enough. Their warm true love for us, and their realization of the joy that awaits us, must drive them on resistlessly. They know, as they never did before, the tremendous issues of human life. They see our dangers clearer than we do. And so they pray for us. Their loud unceasing cry goes up to God for us. Will God not hear that cry? Will He turn away His face and make as though He heard it not? Does He not love to hear it? That ceaseless litany, sung by the souls His grace has saved, and full of faith and hope and love, does it not fall ever sweetly on His ears, and shall it fail of its reward? "The effectual fervent prayer of a righteous man availeth much." What, then, must be the power of the ceaseless prayers of a Paradise full of holy souls? The mind of man cannot measure the blessings God shall give in answer to the prayers of Paradise.

This is no rhapsody, no pious opinion of my own. It is Church Doctrine and Bible Truth. It has always been believed in the Christian Church. All down the ages, through the writings of the greatest teachers of the faith, stretches a long chain of evidence that the saints departed pray for us.[1] The ancient liturgies embody such a belief, and the records of early Christian times show that

[1] The primitive testimony may be most conveniently examined in Bishop Forbes (of Brechin) on the Articles, vol. ii. 381–403.

it was widely held. Although the subject is not treated with fulness in the New Testament, it is alluded to and taken for granted there. Dives in the place of departed spirits is represented as being keenly alive to the dangers of his "five brethren" still in the flesh, and actively exerts himself in their behalf. He appeals to Abraham, as a representative of God, to have them warned of the judgment to come. The logical inference follows from this that the souls in Paradise must be still more anxious for the eternal welfare of those whom they have left on earth, and still more active in exertions on their behalf. Being in the immediate presence of Christ, they go, not to Abraham, but to Him. They enlist in behalf of their friends in the Church Militant on earth the powerful intercessions of the great Captain of their salvation. The anxiety of Dives for the safety of his brethren carries with it an assurance of the affectionate interest and intercession of the saints in Paradise for us who are still upon probation here.

I

In the Revelation of St. John we find several references to the prayers of the saints. He saw in the midst of the throne a Lamb as it had been slain, and He took the book out of the right hand of Him that sat upon the throne, "and when he had taken the book, the four beasts and the four and twenty elders fell down before the Lamb, having every one of them harps, and golden vials full of odours, which are the prayers of the saints" (Rev. v. 6–8). And again he "saw under the altar the souls of them that were slain for the word of God, and for the testimony which they held : and they cried with a loud voice, saying, How long, O God, Holy and True, dost Thou not judge and avenge our blood on them that dwell on the earth?" (Rev. vi. 9, 10). We thus have the testimony of St. John that the souls of the martyrs cry to God in prayer, and that the petitions of departed saints are offered up to Him.

These scriptural references, together with the general consent of the Church, are enough to assure us of the truth that the prayers of the saints at rest are offered up for us.

I hasten on to another question which thrusts itself upon us and must be dealt with here. The saints departed pray for us, but can we ask them for their prayers ? Can we in any sense pray to them ? The Greek and Roman Churches answer that we may, and they use such invocations in their public services and freely in their private prayers. The Anglican Church at the Reformation dropped them from her service-books, and has since then failed to recommend their use. Let us examine into the merits of the case.

When we turn to the Bible we find no reference to such prayers. They are neither commanded nor prohibited ; the limits of prayer are not defined. When we search for records of such a practice in the contemporary literature of the Primitive Church, we do not find them earlier than the fourth century. To what extent it had prevailed before that time we cannot tell. Our only certainty is that by the end of that century it was widespread and approved by the highest authorities.[1]

The great Fathers of the Church, who under the guidance of the Holy Spirit defined and promulgated the faith of Christendom in the general councils of that heroic age, who preserved through those perilous times the great Trinity-truths which they had inherited from apostolic hands,— it was from their teaching and example

[1] The custom of that age may be learned from the Church historian Theodoret, writing about the year 435. "The shrines of the martyrs glorious in their victory are grand, magnificent, conspicuous in size, manifoldly adorned, and sending forth flashes of beauty.   To these, not once or twice in the year, nor even five times, do we go, but oftentimes we hold solemn assemblies, and often every day offer hymns to their Lord ; and those who are in health beg for the preservation of their health ; those who are wrestling with any sickness ask a riddance from their sufferings ; the childless men ask for offspring, and the barren women for children. Those who have gained this gift ask that their gifts may be preserved perfect ; and those who are setting out upon any journey implore them to become their fellow-travellers and guides on the way ; and those who have gained their return offer acknowledgment of the favour ; drawing nigh to them not as gods, but approaching them as devout men and beseeching them to be intercessors on their behalf."—*Græc. Affec. Cur.*, viii.

that the Church learned to invoke the
prayers of the saints in Paradise. When
their teaching was challenged by the heathen
world, they defended it on the ground that
such prayers had been so evidently and
abundantly answered as to prove that they
were in accordance with the will of God.
The Christian world accepted the evidence
as conclusive, and such prayers prevailed
thenceforth throughout the Church. Their
scope and character, however, were strictly
defined and limited. The Fathers were at
great pains to guard their teaching from
misconstructions.[1] They made it plain that
the cultus of the saints in Paradise did not
differ from that of the saints on earth. Their
petitions were the same in kind as those
which they addressed to each other here.
They simply asked that the prayers of
Paradise might be united with their own.
Since their day there has grown up within
the Roman communion a vast practical

[1] See quotations from them in Bishop Forbes (of Edin-
burgh), *Considerationes Modestæ*, 199.

system of invocation inconsistent with the
doctrine and practice of the early Church,
and lacking any definite authority.[1]   This
system uses language which seems to attri-
bute to the saints powers and prerogatives
which encroach upon the mediatorial office
of Christ, which represents them as more
approachable than He, and offers to them
some of the worship which is due to God
alone.   In regard to one of the saints, the
Blessed Virgin Mary, it has gone to startling
lengths.   It represents that "God has re-
signed into her hands (if one might say so)

[1] Although freely and quasi-officially taught, and undis-
tinguished by multitudes of the uninformed from the doctrines
which are of faith, it has never been authoritatively affirmed,
and in fact the Council of Trent deliberately stopped short
of it.   That council contented itself with the declaration
that "it is good and useful suppliantly to invoke the saints,
and to have recourse to their prayers, help, and assistance,
to obtain favours from God, through His Son Jesus Christ
our Lord, who is alone our Redeemer and Saviour."   The
Catechism of the Council still further defines that "God and
the saints are not to be prayed to in the same manner, for
we pray to God that He Himself would give us good things
and deliver us from evil things ; but we beg of the saints
that they would be our advocates, and obtain from God what
we stand in need of."

His omnipotence in the sphere of grace;" that "our salvation is in her hand;" that "God has determined to give us no grace except through the hands of Mary;" that "it is safer to seek salvation through her than directly from Jesus;" that "it is impossible for any to be saved who turns away from her or is disregarded by her, or to be lost who turns to her and is regarded by her."[1] It was against this doctrinal distortion and the excesses resulting from it in the popular teaching and practice of the Roman Church, rather than against her dogmatic decrees, that our twenty-second Article of Religion was aimed. The earlier and purer doctrine of the post-Nicene age, namely, that of *prayer for prayer*, the *Ora pro nobis* of the old service-books, has never been condemned in any part of the Church Catholic.[2] It was held by many

---

[1] These statements and many like them may be found in Liguori's *Glories of Mary*, whose author is one of the approved writers of the Church of Rome.

[2] This was the judgment of the reforming Bishops of the Church of England, as expressed in the Necessary Doctrine

leaders of the Reformation on the Continent,
and has been strongly urged by some of the
best Anglican divines. While it is no longer
embodied in our system of public worship,
there is nothing to hinder us from carrying
it into effect in our private prayers.[1] While
we do not suppose that the saints in Paradise
are directly cognizant of what is said or done
by us, we are led to think that our Lord
reveals to them so much of it as is best for
them to know, and makes them aware of our
desire to be remembered in their prayers.
So long as their mediation is not invoked
like that of Christ, and is understood to be

and Erudition for any Christian Man, which was set forth
under their authority. "To pray unto the saints to be intercessors with us and for us to our Lord in our suits which we
make unto Him, and for such things as we can obtain of
none but Him, so that we esteem not or worship not them
as givers of those gifts, but as intercessors for the same, is
lawful and allowed by the Catholic Church." The same
was maintained by Bishop Andrewes and others later on.

[1] Of course such a practice must be governed by a spirit
of loyalty to our Mother Church, which ought to make us
very cautious about adopting forms of prayer used in other
communions which have departed more widely from primitive
customs than she has thought it safe to go.

one of intercession such as we offer for one
another here, and does not trench upon His
prerogatives, we are not forbidden to think
that the intercession of the saints in Paradise
may as rightly be invoked as that of the
saints on earth. We may safely take our
stand with an eminent Scotch divine, who
(while he prefers the term Advocation)
has learnedly vindicated our right to use
such prayers. His conclusion is: " Let God
alone be religiously adored ; let Him be
prayed to through Christ, who is the only
Mediator, truly and properly speaking, between God and men. Let not the very
ancient custom received in the universal
Church, as well Greek as Latin, of ad-
dressing the saints and angels after the
manner we have mentioned, be condemned
or rejected as impious, nor even as vain or
foolish by the more rigid Protestants. Let
the foul abuses which have crept in be taken
away. And so peace may thereafter easily
be established and sanctioned between the
dissentient parties, as regards this contro-

versy. Which may the God of peace and
of all pious concord vouchsafe to grant for
the sake of His only begotten Son." [1]

Our purpose has been to determine the
relationship which binds the Church in
Paradise to the Church Militant here in earth.
We find it to be a relationship of common
prayer. The Paradise of God is not a silent
land. The prayers of the saints at rest are
ever going up like incense before the throne
of God. They are not selfish prayers. They
are *full of us*, full of our needs as seen in the
larger light of the other world. Perhaps
they may not specify the petty needs of our
daily life, but in the width of their sympa-
thetic interest they are broad enough to
cover all our wants. The boundaries of
human friendship are too narrow to circum-
scribe the prayers of the saints. For every
saint who has been long in Paradise earthly
friendship has long ago ceased to exist. All
whom he knew on earth have departed this
life and gone each to his own place. But

[1] Bishop Forbes, *Considerationes Modestæ*, 313.

he does not cease to pray for those who are
left on earth, although he knew them not in
this life. They are his brethren in the
Church of God, and as such they have his
prayers. Those prayers embrace the whole
great Family of God, and form one of the
strongest bonds to bind it together in the
Communion of Saints.

How good it is to think of the mighty
chorus of prayer which is ever going up from
the saints in Paradise, and which is offered by
our Great High Priest upon the Golden Altar
which is before the Throne! How it must
drown the din of the rude noises of this
unquiet world, and fill the ears of God with
such music as He loves! High above the
faint and faltering notes of our human prayers
it swells, not making them to be unheard,
but reinforcing and accompanying them to
the throne of grace. Together they make a
melody that is only less mighty and less
sweet than the eternal anthem which shall
be sung by all the whole people of God in
the New Jerusalem. I love to think of it,

and try to catch some far-off echo of its harmonies. Sometimes I almost seem to hear it, like the voice of a countless "multitude, and the voice of many waters, and the voice of mighty thunderings," that smites the heart with awe and makes the spirit faint. Sometimes I seem to catch familiar tones amidst its varied harmonies. O God, how sweet they sound! How full of faith, and love, and strong prevailing power, as they plead for us who dwell in solitary homes! Shall not the knowledge that their prayers go up for us give courage and move us mightily to follow on? God grant that in His own good time we may bear our part in the majestic burst of prayer and praise that goes ever up to Him from Paradise, may wait with joy the second coming of our King, and mingle our glad voices in the heavenly singing of our eternal Home!

CHAPTER VI.

WHAT IS OUR RELATIONSHIP TO DEPARTED SAINTS?

ONE of the most talented authoresses of the present day[1] has recently published a book entitled *Max Hereford's Dream*. It is a story, simply and exquisitely told, of our relations to the other world. An orator and philanthropist is struck down, in the noontide of his life, by a lingering disease. He is restless under the enforced quiet of the sick-room. One night he dreams. To his surprise he sees the nursery rhymes of his childhood fulfilled. He sees an angel standing at each corner of his bed.

> " Four corners to my bed,
> Four angels round my head;
> One to watch, two to pray,
> And one to bear my soul away."

---

[1] Edna Lyall.

He wonders why there should be two to pray, and one of the praying angels answers his thought, "I pray for you and for those whom you have influenced who are still upon this earth." Then the other speaks and says, "I pray for those influenced by you who have passed away from this earth." The sick man questions whether it is right to pray for souls in the other world, and to satisfy his questionings the angels lead him forth and show him four scenes.

First they enter a large country house upon which rests the hush of death. Two days before the master of the house was suddenly struck down in the midst of a life of self-indulgence and sin. His faithful wife weeps for him in her sleepless solitude. All the long weary years she has prayed for him, and now death has silenced her prayers. She thinks it wrong to pray for him now, and the thought breaks her heart. *May* she not pray, *must* she not pray for him still?

The angels bear the sick man over land and sea to where from a lofty window the lamp of a solitary student shines. At his writing-table sits a man whom care has made look older than his years. A new sorrow fills his heart to-night. His dearest friend has died and made no sign, acknowledging no faith in God, no hope of future life. With a heavy heart he stifles the prayer-voices that clamour to make themselves heard, and bends over his books.

Just as dawn is breaking, the angels bring their charge to a cottage among the hills. In a tiny room a white-haired labourer lies with wide-open eyes. His lips move in prayer for his children scattered round the world. But most of all he prays for the scapegrace son who died many years ago. A worthless fellow he seemed to all the world, but out of a loving heart full of trust his father prays for him, that, if it be possible, God may have mercy on his soul.

The angels make their last stand before a palace gate. A great sorrow broods within. Beside a bed a child kneels in prayer. The sun's rays make a glory round the bent head

of the boy. Tears, but not of bitterness or
pain, stream down his cheeks. "The rays of
light seen through his wet eyelashes make
tiny rainbows of blue, and red, and yellow,
and the little prince falls to thinking of the
beauty of colour, and of what they have told
him of heaven. Then again he bends his
head and prays with all the fervour of his
childish heart for the brother who has gone
before to the Homeland ; for are they not
still one family above and below ? And why
should the dear name be left out of his
prayers because death has opened the gate
to eternal peace and joy ? "

The sick man goes back to his chamber
with a tranquil heart, for he has learned his
relations, his duty, to the other world. That
is what we want to learn—our relationship to
those who have gone before us into Paradise.
We have found that they remember us, and
think of us, and love us, and pray for us.
How (on our part) do we stand to them ? Do
the relationships which we had to them in life
still exist, or are they broken and brought to

nought? May we pray for those who are gone, or are they beyond the need and the reach of our prayers? These questions remain to be met. Can they be answered so as to bring conviction to our minds and comfort to our hearts? I think they can.

Are the ties of relationship which we form in this life broken and destroyed by death? I find nothing in my reason or in my Bible to make me think so. My mind and my heart assure me that God will not encourage or command the establishment of relationships which must be snapped asunder and reduced to nothingness. The same love which binds together the three Persons of the Blessed Trinity, when God has permitted it to bind human hearts, must be as eternal in the one relationship as in the other. If death makes an utter end of all human ties, it is a cruel, hopeless calamity. If it merely separates for a time those who have such relationships, while the bonds that bind remain unbroken still and their interrupted intercourse shall be renewed again and have full play,

K

then the sharpest sting of death is gone. The
separation God has made for a little time
will but sweeten and enrich the eternal fellowship of kindred hearts. My reason and experience tell me that this must be true. My
Bible confirms what they say. I find nothing
in it which indicates that any pure and good
relationship comes to an end with this life.
It is true that the Bible does not undertake
to tell us with much clearness what new
relationships, if any, will be formed after
death. But I cannot find that it anywhere
says that the pure and holy affections of
earth shall be abolished in Paradise. The
Church, acting as the interpreter of Holy
Writ, has always taught that our human
relationships will exist and be acknowledged
in the future life. And she has always
insisted with especial earnestness upon the
continuance of one relationship, namely, our
fellowship in the Family of God. The
Church Militant on earth and the Church
Expectant in Paradise are vitally and indi-
visibly one. Over and over again in our

Prayer-book this relationship is recognized. Death does not remove one out of the service of the Cross of Christ. It merely transfers him to another department of the service, promotes him to a higher post in the army of God. And so of the other relationships of life, so far as there is genuineness and worth about them. They endure even to the end. Refined, and purified, and spiritualized, they outlast this life and stretch away into the beyond. We must realize that and live up to our responsibilities. Those who have been taken from us into Paradise have claims upon us still. Our thoughts, our good wishes, our loyal devotion, are due to them, as of old. Their hopes, and happiness, and destiny are bound up with ours. We must be true to them, must do our duty as in their sight, must be obedient to their desires for us, remembering that we shall soon render an account of our stewardship to them and to God. We shall do wrong to them and to ourselves, if we forget our mutual membership in God's great Family. The realities of life require us to be mindful of them in all we do. We have the honour of our Family to maintain, even though some of its members be out of sight. Sometime we shall stand by their side, with "all nations, and kindreds, and peoples, and tongues, to be judged" according to the deeds done in the body. Then how good it will be, if we can say that we have been always true to them, true to the uttermost!

In this life one of the strongest bonds that holds together human-kind is the mutual ministry of prayer. Nothing unites us closer to a friend than to pray for him. Nothing stirs us more deeply than to know that some one is praying for us. And when God takes away from us for a time those who have grown dear to us, our most natural impulse is to redouble our prayers for them. The voice of prayer rises into a higher key, and strives to follow them whithersoever they have gone. Our feelings for them have grown tenderer than before, our desires for them are enlarged, we long to commend them to God's loving care. Must we stifle the voices that cry to God out of the depths of our hearts and cease to pray, because death has come between us and them? Is it *right* to ask God's blessing for them at one moment of their existence and *wrong* the next? Is it *ever* wrong to tell God the thoughts and desires of our hearts?

> "Prayer is the soul's sincere desire,
>   Unuttered or exprest."

If, then, our hearts and minds are full of those who have gone out from our midst, and our desires seem to be centred and summed up in them, are we not praying for them anyhow? And ought we not to let God see all that goes on within, ought we not to tell our loving Father *all?*

Such is the natural yearning and reasoning of the human heart. Must it be repressed? Is there anything to forbid us to carry out these natural inclinations which are so strong? To the law and to the testimony. What do our Lord and the Scriptures say? Our Lord says nothing at all, so far as we can find. But does His silence condemn or does it give consent? I think no honest mind can doubt that His silence gives consent. We seem to hear Him say, "I would have told you, if it were not so" (St. John xiv. 2). The Second Book of Maccabees tells us that some two centuries before our Lord became incarnate in the flesh it was customary to pray for the dead.[1] The records of ancient Hebrew life and the testimony of the best Jewish scholars assure us that prayers for the dead were common when He was fulfilling His earthly ministry.[2] In every synagogue they were offered as a matter of course, and are to-day. They formed a part of the Temple worship, where sacrifices were offered for those who had departed this life in a state of imperfect holiness. Under the rules of the Rabbis it was the duty of the son or next of kin to say the Kaddisch, a prayer for the soul of the departed for eleven months after his death.[3] With these beliefs and customs

[1] 2 Macc. xii. 39-end.
[2] See Eisenmenger, *Entdeckt. Judenth.*, ii.
[3] See Dean Plumptre, *The Spirits in Prison*, 267.

our Lord was entirely familiar, but He spoke not one word to condemn them nor to discredit their efficacy. Many of the ways of the Scribes and Pharisees and superstitious outgrowths of their teaching did He condemn with unsparing severity, but these were unblamed by Him. We have no cause to doubt that He and His disciples, loyal as they were to their fathers' ways, joined in them as a part of the worship of the synagogue. In the absence of any word or sign of disapproval, we may be sure they had the sanction of our Lord.

The same reasoning holds good in regard to the first apostles of our Lord. We find no record anywhere that they condemned prayers for the dead. For twelve years after our Lord's Ascension they tarried in Jerusalem and worshipped in the Temple and in synagogues where prayers for the dead were freely used, and their successors believed that they approved of such prayers. Of St. Paul this is particularly true. Surely he who was so swift and stern to condemn the " beggarly

elements" of Pharisaic tradition would not
have spared this custom, if it had run contrary to his principles. Indeed, many of the
best Biblical scholars hold that he actively
practised it. In the Second Epistle to St.
Timothy, speaking of Onesiphorus, who had
befriended him, he exclaims, "The Lord grant
unto him that he may find mercy of the Lord
in that day" (2 Tim. i. 16, 18 ; iv. 19). Now,
it was the unanimous verdict of the early
Fathers, and is the opinion of many of the
best commentators of modern times,[1] that
Onesiphorus had died before St. Paul wrote
to Timothy, and that his words were a prayer
for the dead. If they are right, then we have
scriptural proof that St. Paul not only tacitly
approved of such prayers, but offered them
himself. It would be impossible to prove
that they were not used by all the first
apostles of our Lord. At any rate, it is
certain that their immediate successors, the
Christians of the first two centuries, made
large use of them. The Roman Catacombs

---

[1] Such as Alford, Bengel, Ellicott, Sadler, etc.

show that the practice is at least almost as old as Christianity.[1] The natural inference from their testimony is that from the beginning Christians used the forms of prayer for the dead which they inherited from the Jews. And now we come to a most striking and important fact. All the liturgies of the Primitive Church contain prayers for the dead. Beginning with the second century after Christ, all of them, the liturgies of Jerusalem, Antioch, Alexandria, Rome, Carthage, Gaul, and all the rest, contain such prayers. They make it certain that, beginning soon after the time of Christ, all Christians everywhere were accustomed to pray for departed souls.[2] Such prayers were

[1] Dean Luckock's *After Death* gives a most valuable treatment of these points. See the chapters on the "Testimony of the Catacombs," the "Testimony of the Early Fathers," and the "Testimony of the Primitive Liturgies."

[2] "It is a fact which cannot be gainsaid that *in every one of them*, without exception, there is a commemoration of the faithful departed. The entire universality of the practice must remove any ground for doubt upon the subject. Much has been said about the difficulty of arriving at what the ancients believed, but here over the whole Christian world we have evidence for this truth from the most solemn docu-

the unvarying use of the Church of England
down to Reformation days. Nor did she
then abruptly break off the continuous usage
of fifteen centuries. The first Reformed
Prayer-book contained prayers for the faithful dead, and the evidences which we have
of the prevalence of private prayers modelled
upon them shows that the reformers neither
condemned nor opposed their use. In fact,
the Church distinctly and deliberately refused
to condemn them. As time passed on, the
Lutheran and Calvinistic reformers of the
Continent gained influence in England, and
attempted to shape the English Reformation
in accordance with their own ideas. They
were able to influence, but not to control it.
Moved by their clamour, the English Church
carried the movement further than she would
of her own accord have gone, but there were
bounds beyond which she declined to pass.

ments which may be traced up to the highest antiquity,
documents which with the strongest evidences of a common
origin, yet vary sufficiently to become concurrent testimonies
in favour of any doctrine which they agree in expressing."—
Bishop Forbes on the Articles, Art. xxxi.

Her standard was the doctrine and discipline of the Primitive Church, and below that she would not suffer herself to fall. Amongst other things, the foreign Reformers attacked prayers for the dead, demanding that they should be disused and condemned. To a part of this the Church agreed. She struck out most of them from her service-books, leaving only a few brief petitions of the sort. The result is that in the Prayer-book which we use to-day we find only very slight remembrance of the dead. In our Prayer for the Church Militant we "bless God's holy name for all His servants departed this life in His faith and fear, beseeching Him to give us grace so to follow their good examples, that *with them* we may be partakers of His heavenly kingdom." Again, at the consecration in the Holy Eucharist, we pray that "we and all thy whole Church may obtain remission of our sins, and all other benefits of His Passion." We have the testimony of Bishop Cosin, who was the chief framer of the English Prayer-book in its final form, that the words "and all thy whole Church" were deliberately intended to be a prayer both for the living and the dead.[1] Thus, while our English Reformers yielded much to their Continental brethren, they did not obliterate from our Prayer-book all reference to the dead. But when the foreign Reformers became bolder and demanded that the English Church should authoritatively condemn all prayers for the dead, they struck a rock. When the Articles of Religion were being framed, an effort was made to secure such a result. The twenty-second Article now reads as follows : " The Romish doctrine concerning Purgatory, Pardons, Worshipping and Adoration, as well of Images as of Reliques, and also Invocation of Saints, is a fond thing vainly invented, and grounded upon no warranty of Scripture, but rather repugnant to the Word of God." It ought to be more widely known that in the first draft of that Article, after the word "Pardons," the Puritans

[1] Bishop Cosin's *Works,* vol. v. p. 351, Anglo-Catholic Library.

had inserted "Prayers for the Dead." But after discussion it was struck out, the English Reformers thus deliberately declining to condemn such prayers. In the preface to our Prayer-book they described the first Prayer-book of the English Church, which contained numerous prayers for the dead, as "a very godly order, agreeable to the Word of God and the Primitive Church, and very comfortable to all Christian people desiring to live in Christian conversation." It cannot therefore be said with any show of truth that prayers for the dead have been condemned or forbidden in the Anglican Church. Although we have but a scanty supply of them for public use, there is nothing in the law of the Church to hinder us from using them privately as largely as we please.

I have left till the last the *efficacy* of prayers for the dead. The question is a double one: What is accomplished by such prayers, and for whom may we offer them?

One of the popular difficulties of our times

is to understand how such prayers can benefit those whose earthly life is at an end.   If you believe that their probation-time is past and that they are at rest in Paradise, why do you pray for them ?   So the world asks us.   We reply, Yes, we know that they are at rest, we suppose that their time of proba- tion is fulfilled, that they have entered on their reward.   But they are not made per- fect yet.   They still need blessings from the hand of God.   They need to be purified and drawn closer to Him day by day, and there will come a time when they with us must stand before their Judge.   There is, therefore, much which we may ask of God for them. The blessings of rest, and peace, and spiritual growth in Paradise ; the shining of a per- petual light ; an entrance into the know- ledge of God ; the enjoyment of full com- munion with the saints ; a joyful resurrection of their bodies from the grave ; and a merciful judgment in the great day of God ; —these things they need, and our hearts prompt us to ask these gifts for them from

God. I know that God desires and intends that they shall have all these things in His own good time, but so He always did, even while they were alive on earth. I know that they are in God's hands now, but so they always were, and so are we. So far as God's willingness to give is concerned, there is no need that we should ask anything from Him, for them, or for ourselves, or for any one. God does not *need* our prayers, but He loves to hear them none the less. There is no virtue in them, except that God is a loving Father who wants us to come to Him and ask in childlike faith the things which His own nature prompts Him to give. He anticipates our prayers, and all of them are but the reflection of the mind of God in us. Whatever, then, we desire, for ourselves, for others, or for the dead, we are to ask in simple childlike faith, leaving Him to answer as He will.

But may we pray for all the dead, for those who we fear have lost their souls, for such as have "died and made no sign"?

Yes, if our desires for them are pure, and if we pray in accord with the Christian law of prayer—" Nevertheless not my will, but Thine, be done "—we may. Our Father, who is tenderer than the tenderest of mankind, would not have us hide our hearts from Him. His mercy is larger than we can think. I do not fear to say that it will save more souls than our most tender mercy would embrace. While the formal intercessions of the Church are only offered for the faithful departed, those who have died in her communion, our private prayers may take a wider range. We need not fear to cherish faith, broad and deep and strong, in the saving power of our Redeemer, Christ. We must not doubt the results of the eternal sacrifice of Him, " who would have all men to be saved." [1] So long as we do

[1] There is an extensive literature of modern times, of which Archdeacon Farrar's *Eternal Hope* may be taken as a representative, against which we must be somewhat on our guard. In its eagerness to encourage the wider hope that the majority of mankind may somehow be saved, it not only maintains that there may be a probation after death, but its loose language sometimes seems to imply that catholic theology has heretofore doomed the mass of mankind to

not know the exact degree of impenitent resist-
ance which may deprive any soul of the salvation which Christ has purchased for it, we need
not cease to pray.   After we have laboured

eternal loss.   Such an implication is not warranted by facts.
It is true that Calvinism, which has no doubt been adopted
in times past by some members of the Church, does demand
such a belief. But the Church Catholic has never com-
mitted herself to a conclusion so abhorrent to all the better
instincts of humanity, and which our Lord distinctly declined
to affirm (St. Luke xiii. 23, 24).   While she has not
ventured to teach that there will be a probation after death,
she has left men free to hope that many, both in heathen
and Christian lands, of whom in our limited charity we
should despair, may "find mercy in that day." "To infer
from the doctrine that all men who die in a certain condition,
of which Omniscience alone can take infallible cognizance in
any given case, are eternally excluded from the vision of God,
that therefore the great majority of men do actually die in
that unhappy condition, is about as reasonable as to conclude
that because Christ died for all men, therefore all men must
necessarily be saved."—Oxenham, *Catholic Eschatology*, 25.

Dr. Pusey wrote near the close of his life (see preface to
Eternal Hope), " I do strongly hope that the great mass of
mankind will be saved, all whom God could save without
destroying their free agency.   He does not treat us like
stocks and stones, but as beings whom He has endowed with
the power freely to love Him.   But since God has only
spoken of His will to save us, and has not said whether
mankind will accept that will for theirs, I could have no
belief on the subject.   I leave it blindly to the hands of
God."

L

in this life for the salvation of those whom
we love, if we still halt between hope and
fear for them, we may pray for them still.
With true unfaltering love and faithfulness
we may plead with God, even to the end,
that, if it be possible, they may be saved.
What may be His answer I cannot tell, but
that He would have us "pray without
ceasing" I do know. It would be a cruel
wrong if He would not let His children tell
Him all the desires and sorrows of their
hearts. And surely He who in His earthly
life was so quick to hear and answer every
cry of needy souls, who dealt so tenderly
with all human want and woe, who mingled
his tears with those who wept about the
grave of Lazarus, surely He will sympathize
with every longing of our hearts, "unuttered
or exprest." *To* Him and *through* Him,
then, let us pray for all who have departed
this life:—for such as we humbly hope are
in Paradise, that He will grant them an
eternal rest and let perpetual light shine
upon them, "brightening ever more and more

unto the perfect day;" and for those for whom our conscience is afraid, that in His tender mercy and compassionate love He may do with them as seemeth to Him good.

CHAPTER VII.

WHAT IS THE RELATIONSHIP OF ALL SAINTS TO GOD?

THE foregoing chapters have been occupied with the "comfortable doctrine" of the blessed communion and fellowship existing between all the whole people of God both in the seen and unseen worlds. My aim has been to give as clear a view of the whole subject as was possible, and to make a frank and faithful statement of the teaching of the Bible and the Church. If I have erred at any point, may God pardon me and overrule my mistakes for good. It has seemed to me of the utmost importance that the scope, and strength, and sacredness of our Christian relationships should be known and recognized. A living belief in them is a part of the Christian Faith. A faithful observance of the duties which they involve is an essential element of Christian life.

But our theme is not exhausted yet. The saints have communion, not only nor chiefly with each other, but above all and through all and in all with God. Without Him there could be no fellowship between the saints. He has made all the strong and sacred relationships which hold them together. He cements them; He binds them fast; He makes them to endure. Without Him they would all drop apart and be as though they had not been. The Communion of Saints is sustained and vitalized by Him. But what it remains for me to insist upon is this: that the Communion of Saints is not simply between men, but between men and God; is not chiefly a fellowship of the saints with each other, but of the saints with Christ. The bands which bind together the children of the great Family of God, stretch on and up to the Throne and tie us fast to the Father and the Elder Brother there. The strongest of our relationships, the sweetest and the best of them, are those that exist between us and God. Close and warm and constant as are the intimacies between us and our brethren in the Household of Faith, they need not lessen our loving loyalty to the great Head of the House. Our intercourse with Him should gather up into itself all other fellowships that they may ripen in the sunshine of His love. Children love one another none the less because they love father and mother more. But the great love which comes back to them binds the little lives together and enlarges their capacity for mutual love. Take away the father and mother love from the life of Home, and where shall the affections of childhood appear? Just so it is in the great Family of God. The children must esteem one another very highly in love, but the inspiration of that love is to be found in God. "This is My commandment, That ye love one another, as I have loved you" (St. John xv. 12). Until we learn something of the great love of God for us, and there has been some outflow of love to Him, our human loves will be but weak and imperfect at the best.

The Communion of the Saints with God, then, is an important subject for us to think upon. Let us ask ourselves such questions as these : Who can be said to have communion with God ? How is their communion realized, and to what extent can it go?

First, who are in communion with God ? I answer, all the saints, all who have been baptized and are in any true sense followers of Christ. All such are related to God by a near and true relationship. They are His children and have all the privileges and responsibilities which belong to them as such. However imperfectly their rights may be realized and their duties done, the fact remains. They are "members of Christ, the children of God, and inheritors of the Kingdom of Heaven." Their fellowship with God may hardly be a conscious one, they may not comprehend how close they have come to Him, they may yet have much to learn of Him, but that does not alter their relationship. Nor does that relationship depend upon their continuance in this life. It is neither interrupted nor broken by death. The saints in Paradise find themselves brought closer to God than before. Most of the hindrances to their full communion with Him are now removed. They are growing day by day in devout nearness to Him. They cannot be any more truly children of God than they were before, but they comprehend more perfectly what it is to be His children now. God does not love them more now than He did before, but they have gained new capacity to feel His love and to love Him in return. Their entrance into the unseen has wakened into a more vigorous activity the affections which had been more or less stifled here. Their communion with God is growing fuller, deeper, and more satisfying every day. All the saints of God, then, whether living in this world or in Paradise, are joined in one communion and fellowship with Him.

But how is this communion brought about, in what does it consist? It has two sides which complete and supplement each other, a Godward and a manward side. It consists chiefly, on the one side, in the communication of a divine supernatural life from God to men; on the other, in the offering of an individual and united worship by men to God. Let us consider these two aspects of it separately.

First, as God's contribution to the Communion of the Saints with Him, there is a gift of divine and heavenly life from Him. Christianity is not a system of doctrines to be believed. It is a new and higher *life to be lived*, an unworldly supernatural life. We cannot originate it ourselves. We cannot sustain and develop it of ourselves. God must give it to us as He did our natural life, and, like our natural life, it must be fed and nourished by Him, or it will fail.[1] This

---

[1] "We make more progress in one year when we have learned to receive life from Christ, than in a whole lifetime of struggling by ourselves. It must be so; for Jesus Christ has said, 'Without Me ye can do nothing.' Ninety-nine out of a hundred of those whom I have to help, individually, shipwreck themselves on this rock; they are struggling to

spiritual life He plants within us at the
baptismal font.   He strengthens and renews
it by the gift of the Holy Ghost in confirma-
tion.   He feeds it with the Bread which came
down from Heaven, the Bread of Life, as
often as we kneel at the altar rail.   At every
communion which we make we receive a new
supply of spiritual vitality from Christ.   At
every participation in the sacred mysteries
the superhuman life of Christ is poured into
us, so that He lives in us and we in Him.[1]
This is no theory.   It is the simple truth as
stated by our Lord Himself.   "I am the
living Bread which came down from heaven :
if any man eat of this Bread, he shall live for

make themselves better instead of opening their hearts to
receive.   And so they multiply their difficulties a thousand-
fold.   They are like a man who, instead of opening the
windows of his house in the morning, should resolve to light
up every corner of it by his own unaided efforts !   He will
succeed in making a sort of light, at last ; but how different
from that which comes simply according to the law of God's
creation, by opening wide the windows and letting the sunlight stream in ! "—Bishop Wilkinson, *The Communion of
Saints*, p. 44.

[1] Compare the Prayer of Humble Access in the Communion Office.

ever : and the Bread which I will give is My
flesh, which I will give for the life of the
world. Verily, verily, I say unto you, Except
ye eat the flesh of the Son of Man, and drink
His blood, *ye have no life in you*" (St. John
vi. 51–53). Christ, then, is the Source, the
Fountain-head from which we draw our life
as saints, and His sacraments are the chan-
nels through which it flows into us. The
communication of that life is His share in the
Communion of Saints. It is given to all who
are called to be saints in such degree as they
are willing to receive. Planted and nourished
in them "now in the time of this mortal life,"
it is carried on into Paradise.[1]   We must not
think of our eternal life as something not yet
begun. It began at our baptism. It is going
on now. We have entered into life. Christ

---

[1] "Where the Sacred Body lieth
        Eagle-souls will congregate ;
  Who with saints and happy angels,
        Thus their spirits recreate ;
  One same Living Bread sustaining
        Denizens of either state."
(From Peter Damiani's Hymn on the Glory of Paradise,
translated by Dr. Neale.)

lives in us, and His life can never end. So the Christian life which we have begun to live is an eternal life, which will endure in Paradise, being perfected in us there, and go on in Heaven. It is this life, given us by Christ and continued throughout eternity, which thrills through the whole company of the saints, binding them to one another and to God.

Such is God's part in the Communion of the Saints with Him. Now, what do the saints render to God on their part? The answer occurs to us in beautiful and significant words, fragrant with the memory of those who taught them to us years ago. "Our duty towards God is to believe in Him, to fear Him, and to love Him with all our heart, with all our mind, with all our soul, and with all our strength; to worship Him, to give Him thanks, to put our whole trust in Him, to call upon Him, to honour His Holy Name and His Word, and to serve Him truly all the days of our life." But, looked at in the light of time and eternity, this "whole duty of man" may be comprehended in one word, *worship.* Worship is the chief occupation of all the saints of God. It is one of the natural instincts of the human heart. I cannot bring myself to despise the ignorant idolater who bows down before his block of wood or stone. I reverence him. I recognize in him something antagonistic to the proud spirit of this age—a mysterious God-implanted instinct of reverent devotion, a blind groping after God, which tells me that he is a brother-man and has a soul. The desire and the capacity to worship distinguishes man above the brutes and testifies to his kinship with God. The most natural occupation, then, the most absorbing pursuit, the highest joy of the saints, is to worship God. To glorify Him is their most ravishing delight. What loftier, nobler enjoyment could they have than to show their admiration and reverence for a Being infinitely holier than themselves! Before the triune God and the sacred mystery of the Eternal Sacrifice they love to bow, and sometimes silently adore and sometimes lift glad songs of praise.

" O ye servants of the Lord, bless ye the Lord,
  Praise Him and magnify Him for ever.
  O ye spirits and souls of the righteous, bless ye the Lord,
  Praise Him and magnify Him for ever."

The "servants of the Lord" on earth render
but a feeble and faltering offering of worship
to their God. In so far as their infirmities
permit, they do worship Him. But with
"the spirits and souls of the righteous," the
saints in Paradise, it is far different. Their
worship goes ever up before the throne. It
echoes always in the ears of God.[1]   The

---

[1] "When, in that noble hymn in our morning service,
alike laudatory and commemorative, we declare that the
glorious company of the Apostles, the goodly fellowship of
the Prophets, the noble army of Martyrs, and the holy
Church throughout all the world, *praise the Lord*,—are we
uttering mere unmeaning words? Are we using language
merely figurative and symbolical? If we know that in some
portions of our service of praise we use words in which
angels glorify their Creator, yea, if we are sure that we are
permitted to utter accents that day and night are sounding
in the courts of heaven, which the most transcendent order
of created beings, the mystical four that surround the
eternal throne, are pouring forth in ceaseless adoration;—if
we are one with angels, and archangels, and all the company
of heaven, in ascribing praise and honour to Him that was,
and is, and is to come, can the holy dead be silent in that
universal hymn?"—Bishop Ellicott, *Destiny of the Creature*,
130.

constant occupation, the business, of the saints in Paradise is to worship God. There is nothing to distract them from that one pursuit, nothing to hinder them from worshipping. Worship is their joy, their delight, their life. I wish we might realize something of the glorious worship which breaks ever round the throne of God. From vast cathedral piles, from many a humbler town and village church, from temples not made with hands, from countless solitary hearts, it rises day by day. From Paradise in clearer, loftier strains it swells, a majestic ceaseless melody, sweeter and grander than mortal ears have ever heard. While high above all, and blending all earth's voices into heavenly harmony that thrills the universe, the sound of golden harps is mingled with the glorious voice of myriad angel-hosts that gather round about the Throne. The universe has been described [1] as a Temple, a vast cathedral, made without hands, for the worship of the great Bishop and Shepherd of our souls.

[1] Bellett, *The Dead in Christ*, 98.

Its nave, its outer court, is the Church on earth. Its chancel, its holy place, is the gardens of Paradise. Its sanctuary, its holy of holies, is the hallowed place about the great white throne. From every part of this glorious temple of our God goes up the one unending chorus of harmonious praise which living saints and dead, and angels and archangels, sing. O God, attune our ears and prepare our hearts that we may hear the majestic worship of Thine universe, and make us love to take our humble part in it!

Our final question is, What are the limits of the Communion of the Saints with God? How far can it go?

In this our earthly life it cannot go so far as we would wish. It is limited by the littleness of our capacity, and hindered by our love for the things which are seen. We know so little about God, even at the best; so many things come between us and Him, that our worship is feeble, and inconstant, and incomplete. The atmosphere which surrounds us is too thick with the mists and shadows which rise out of human life for us to catch a clear view of God. If we could see Him as He is, no doubt we should fall down before Him and adore. But our eyes are holden, so that we cannot plainly see Him, and so they will be to the end of this life. The worship of the saints on earth will always be a faltering and fragmentary thing. But, imperfect as it is, it must not be despised. It is the sweetest and best thing in human life. It is the highest act of which we are capable. It is the noblest employment of the soul, the heavenliest thing that we can do. The most ecstatic moments of our lives are those in which we see beyond the cloud-lands of human sin and get faint glimpses of the glory of God. The most precious hours are those we spend in conscious fellowship with the great Unseen. The highest, holiest act of human life is when we kneel beside the altar rail and open wide our hearts that the life of God may be poured in and fill them "up to the brim." With all its limitations, in all its littleness, the worship of

M

Almighty God is the best thing in all the world.

If the worship of earth is so blessed a thing, what must be the communion of the saints with God in Paradise? Set free from all the powers of sin, lifted out of all the entanglements of life in the flesh, brought into the nearer presence of their Lord, their spiritual gaze is turned ever towards God. No longer darkly as in a glass, nor dimly from afar, they see His face. In the piercing light which shines from that face the mysteries of life are melting fast away, and they are learning to look into the bottomless depths of the knowledge of God.[1] Their vision is not perfect

[1] "The Beatific Vision of God in Christ will have the power to transform those who are admitted to it, in proportion to their power of taking it in. As it will be perpetually before their eyes, and they will never for an instant lose sight of it again, their power of taking it in will be perpetually increased; and they, in consequence, will still in heaven be more and more 'transformed into the same image from glory to glory.' All will not be accomplished at the first glance. It is only true up to a certain point to say that the day of faith and hope will be over, because they are swallowed up in sight. Faith and hope, like charity, are among the things which will 'abide,' even when the saints

yet. The power has not yet been given them to see the full brightness of His face. Neither we nor they could bear it now; we could not "see God and live." Even the thought of seeing Him is overwhelming now. To behold His face; to gaze upon that Beauty of which all fair things are but shadows, or at best but faint reflected rays; to stand ever in that light which so lightens the city of God that there is "no need of the sun, neither of the moon, to shine in it," for the Light of the World is the light thereof; to have that light streaming upon the mysteries of our human life, illuminating them in the everlasting noontide of an unclouded day; to see with the eyes of the soul the supreme moral beauty, the

know as they were known, because there will always remain an infinity of blessed experience to be drawn from that inexhaustible fountain of goodness; and as age passes after age, it will seem to the redeemed as if they were only just beginning to appreciate the glory of God, and only just beginning to be capable of appreciating it. The eternal life of the saints consists in the knowledge of God, in heaven as on earth, and there is no limit which we are aware of at which that eternal life will cease to expand and increase in strength."—Canon Mason, *Faith of the Gospel.*

beauty of holiness, truth, and love, unbroken
by any earthborn cloud, gazing upon and being
transformed into the likeness of it eternally ;
to see the Glorified Manhood of the Son of
God ; to look upon that very Body in which
our Saviour dwelt on earth, which was raised
from the grave, "the firstfruits of them that
slept," the first human body to enter Heaven
and stand by the throne of God, and which
with its glorified scars now pleads for us
there ; to advance ever into that awful but
blissful Presence wherein the All-Holy Trinity
abides through all eternity and take up our
abode in it ; to be at Home with God ;—this is
almost more than we can hope or think.   It
is the chief end of man, the consummation of
our Christian life, the loftiest height of human
happiness.   The dawn of the Beatific Vision
upon the soul is the sweet opening of an endless joy, which, deepening and penetrating it
ever more and more, increases throughout
that long day upon which the sun shall no
more go down.   " The path of the just is as
the shining light, which shineth more and

more unto the Perfect Day," the eternal
Easter Day when God shall lead His ransomed people Home.   Then shall His might
and majesty be clearly seen, and every desire
of the heart of man be more than satisfied in
an endless and unhindered Communion of
the Saints with one another and with God.

"O Christ, our Refuge and Strength, Thou
Hope of humankind, whose light shineth from
afar upon the dark clouds which hang
around us : behold Thy redeemed ones cry
unto Thee, Thy banished ones whom Thou hast
redeemed with Thine own most precious
blood.   Hear us, O God our Saviour, Thou
who art the Hope of all the ends of the earth,
and of them that remain in the broad sea.
We are tossed about on the wild and stormy
waves in the dark night ; and Thou, standing
on the eternal shore, beholdest our peril ; save
us for Thy Name's sake.   Guide us among the
shoals and quicksands which beset all our
course, and bring us at length in safety to the
Haven where we would be.

"O bright and glorious day, which knows

no evening, whose sun shall no more go down, in which I shall hear the voice of praise, the voice of joy and thanksgiving, Thy voice saying unto me, 'Enter thou into the joy of thy Lord;' enter into joy everlasting, into the House of the Lord thy God, where are things great and unsearchable, and wonderful things without number; where life shall be calm, and glad, and thrilling; where is settled and supreme security, and tranquil joy, and joyful happiness, a happy eternity, an eternal blessedness, the Blessed Trinity, the Unity in Trinity, the Trinity in Unity, the blissful vision of the Godhead, the joy of the Lord.

"O everlasting Kingdom, Kingdom of endless ages, whereon rests the untroubled light and peace of God, which passeth all understanding, where the souls of the Saints are at rest, and everlasting joy is upon their heads, and sorrow and sighing have fled away! Oh, how glorious is the Kingdom in which all Thy Saints reign with Thee, O Lord, clothed with light as with a garment, and having on their heads a crown of precious stones! For there is infinite unfading joy, gladness without sorrow, health without a pang, life without toil, light without darkness, life without death; there the vigour of age knows no decay, and beauty withers not, nor doth love grow cold, nor joy wane away, for there we look evermore upon the Face of the Lord God of Hosts." [1]

[1] St. Augustine, *Soliloquies of the Soul to God*, xxxv., translated in the *Treasury of Devotion*.

PRINTED BY WILLIAM CLOWES AND SONS, LIMITED, LONDON AND BECCLES.